JACOB FUGGER THE RICH

Merchant and Banker of Augsburg, 1459–1525

by

Jacob Strieder
Professor of Economic History
University of Munich

Translated by
Mildred L. Hartsough
Associate in Research in Business History

Edited by
N. S. B. Gras
Straus Professor of Business History

Graduate School of Business Administration
Harvard University

▽

ARCHON BOOKS
1966

To His Highness
the Prince
KARL ERNST FUGGER-GLÖTT

EDITOR'S INTRODUCTION

Jacob Fugger is a splendid example of the successful merchant who flourished shortly after the discovery of America. The biography of Fugger by Professor Strieder is also a fine example of the work done by economic historians in the field that is becoming specialized as business history. Other economic historians who have been interested in the business man are Ehrenberg and Sombart in Germany, Sée in France, and Unwin in England.

The present book and others by the same author are helping to lay the foundations for business history. The study of economic history has become so well developed that no one can comprehend it all. Those who wish to make progress in the field actually specialize in some part of it—financial, commercial, industrial, or agricultural history, or the history of economic regulation, or the history of prices, wages, rent, and income. It may be a matter of lingering regret that subjects and disciplines are being so split up, but it is also a matter of congratulation, because intelligent specialization means progress in the discovery of facts and in the formulation of generalizations.

In the early history of the business of getting a living no step was more important than the development of a class of entrepreneurs. A middle class of profit-takers came upon the scene to rival and often to command princes, ecclesiastics, nobles, artisans, and peasants. The coming of this class was, of course, unplanned. As the noble found his setting in the castle, the peasant in the field, and the cleric in the pulpit, so did the business man flourish in the town. There protection could be found, special services were available, and a system of economic regulation could be worked out favorable to trade.

Today we accept the business man, large and small, as part of our civilization; and nowhere is this more true than in America. But historically we must account for him: he has arrived late upon the scene. In each great epoch of civilization he has come with the town and in all but ours he has gone down with the town.

A social class is a bundle of habits and attitudes, a multicolored pattern of ways of doing things and of values in life. The business man was foresighted, continuously active, rational rather than emotional in his attitudes, saving his income for further investment, diversifying these investments, and risking his capital for the sake of profits. That the buying and selling of goods and credit came at times to be an end in itself is to be expected.

Just what forces were at work to create such a class of business men and such an individual as Fugger is a problem not easy to decide. It has been thought that Judaism and Calvinism were influential while Catholicism was not helpful in the creation of a spirit of enterprise. Certainly the Jews and the Scots have been excellent business men, as also Baptists and Presbyterians. The Huguenots in France and the Puritans in New England were hard workers and successful artisans and traders. Jacob Fugger was a Catholic and also a great merchant, but a large part of his success in business was due to his breaking away from the Church's attitude to interest and just price. In fact, he may be regarded as one of the forces within the Church that led to a reformed Catholic attitude to business.

Much more important than religion is the existence of individualism and initiative among men, founded upon deep psychological considerations. Individualism was in no sense new when the medieval town was developing: it had existed in the person of the marauding leader of a pillaging band and in religious leaders and saints. But at last there was opportunity for commanding leadership on a large scale and on a peaceful and rational basis. The trade within towns and between towns and fairs was the favorable setting for the business man's birth. It was partly the cause and partly the result of his activity, just as Augsburg was partly the cause and partly the result of the life and work of Jacob Fugger.

The use of money and the bill of exchange was necessary to business success, as were many other things such as a business ethics, bookkeeping, and a development of the applied arts. In the affairs of Jacob Fugger we find many coins in use, the most prominent in commercial reckoning being the gold gulden.

Although the gold or Rhenish gulden varied in weight and fineness from time to time, it was roughly equivalent to the English pound sterling about the year 1500. The English pound would have purchased about 25 bushels of the best wheat at the same time. Since wheat is worth about $1.00 a bushel (? 1930), we can say that the purchasing power of the gold gulden, reckoned in terms of the best American wheat, would be about $25.00. Accordingly, it would·not be far wrong to multiply by 25 the various figures that are expressed in gold gulden in the chapters that follow, in order to get the equivalent in American dollars. Of course, any such statement as this, based upon consideration of the price of only one commodity, may be far from satisfactory in general application.

The form of business combination used by the Fuggers was the family partnership. This, along with the temporary partnership which developed in Genoa, was an important link in the chain which led from the individual business man to the joint-stock company and finally the corporation holding various other corporations together. The great problems in family partnership were to provide for continuity of effort and capacity in management. Jacob Fugger was insistent upon both. The outstanding modern instance of a family partnership is the Rothschilds. A notable instance nearer home is the Straus brothers of the R. H. Macy & Company, Inc., New York, who, although they now operate under a corporate form, have been essentially a family partnership.

The business of the Fuggers was centralized in the home office at Augsburg, but somewhat localized in such distant points as Naples and Antwerp. The Fugger inventory of 1527 illustrates the wide-flung nature of the business in which the partners of Augsburg were engaged. When the family partners or the partners and their children were numerous and capable, there were plenty of satisfactory district managers, as we should say. But otherwise there must have been a trying problem to find men of ability and integrity to occupy subordinate positions of such importance.

Jacob Fugger and his kinsmen were non-specialized merchants. They were like John Hancock and Stephen

Girard in America. Primarily buyers and sellers on a wholesale basis, they reached out on the one side to banking and on the other to the control of production. This was typical of the big business men of the. period from the twelfth to the early nineteenth century.

The Fuggers, though not so much Jacob as his ancestors, were merchants who both bought cloth and controlled its manufacture under the wholesale handicraft system. In such a business the foundations of the family fortunes were laid. In the buying and selling of cloth and other wares little distinction was probably made between wholesale and retail trade, though the former was emphasized as the more lucrative. From the trade in ore—especially copper and silver— the Fuggers extended their activities until they came into the control of mines. These were ordinarily operated by smaller people who took the contract and with it the active control and much or all of the risk.

Jacob Fugger assisted private individuals by loaning them money and transferring credit. He was, indeed, a private banker, receiving deposits, making loans, changing coins, and buying and selling bills of exchange. To churchmen he made loans to aid them in buying preferment. He transferred papal taxes to Rome and made loans to the popes. For his part in the collection of the revenues from the sale of indulgences he was right roundly condemned. In so far as the sale of indulgences was one of the factors in the Reformation, and in so far as the proceeds were to assist in building St. Peter's Cathedral in Rome, we see that Fugger was one of the links between the Italian Renaissance and the Protestant Reformation.

Jacob Fugger's most dramatic act was the financing of the election of the Emperor Charles v. To bring this about, in the face of the rivalry of Francis i of France, a great deal of ready cash and solid credit were required. The electors had to be bribed in a princely fashion. Jacob Fugger was at hand to aid not only the petty tradesman and peasant seeking an indulgence but also the great churchman and the lay electors when about to perform a public duty for private profit. The significance of the deed for Europe and for civilization can be appreciated when we realize that the Holy Roman Empire and Spain with the Netherlands and the colonies were brought together in one great political combination. Much of later history was the undoing of Fugger's act of 1519.

The business policy of this astute merchant is worthy of careful study. He sought to keep the partnership within the family but to keep it virile and effective. He aimed at profits such as the medieval Church would never have sanctioned. The profits that come from monopoly on a large scale were several times attempted and with no qualms of conscience, for the large losses incident to trade had to be balanced by large gains. There was no power in Europe or in Christendom that could gainsay a merchant in such a strategic position as that occupied by Jacob Fugger.

Through his assistance to Charles v, Jacob Fugger allied himself with the Empire and with Spain and against France. In this way he lost all chances of developing counters in Lyons and Paris, but he opened up possibilities in Spain and in the Spanish colonies. On the whole, however, Jacob Fugger was more inclined to emphasize the business of a Middle Europe than he was to venture far overseas. His investment in real estate in the breast of Europe shows not only the focus of his imagination but a desire for the safety that comes from diversification and the distinction that comes from landed property.

Jacob Fugger was a merchant not a saint, a business man not a reformer. In so far as he challenged the Church's stand in the matter of just price and no "interest," however, he may be said to be the first of modern business men. But in so far as he was nonspecialized in function, he belongs to an order that has quite passed away in advanced countries of the world. His various functions have been taken over by different classes—wholesalers, retailers, manufacturers, common carriers, and bankers. In a sense, the class of merchants to which Jacob Fugger belonged was the father of them all.

As we began by indicating that Fugger had an able biographer, so we may conclude by adding that the biographer has an able translator. Just as the author sought to state simply the gist of the story of Fugger's life as a business man, so the translator has endeavored to follow, not to embellish, the original presentation.

AUTHOR'S INTRODUCTION

JACOB FUGGER AND THE FUGGER PERIOD IN THE HISTORY
OF GERMAN COMMERCE

This book is not an attempt at an exhaustive biography of Jacob Fugger the Rich; it is designed rather as an essay in economic history. The four hundredth anniversary, on December 30, 1925, of the death of this greatest of German merchants was the immediate occasion for its preparation and publication by the author, who, as professor of economic history at the University of Munich, had long had a special interest in the study of the old commercial families of southern Germany, and of the House of Fugger in particular. The source material for the study of the life and work of Jacob Fugger is extraordinarily scanty. To the historian he lives almost exclusively in his deeds; for his character, his views, the guiding principles which made him an outstanding example of the capitalistic entrepreneur of Europe in the early modern period, we must depend largely upon inference from the actual facts of his life. In the portrait of Fugger here presented, chief emphasis has been placed—in contrast to all earlier biographies—upon fitting him and his accomplishments properly into the milieu of German and of European economic development. Only in this way can we of the present find a vantage point from which we can completely understand and evaluate his personality and his achievements. The term milieu must here be taken in its wider sense of including all those factors which influence the development of a great man.

For Jacob Fugger, three spheres of varying radius were of decisive importance. The widest of these reached to Italy. Unless we keep continually in mind the Italians as the most progressive merchants of the Middle Ages, we shall never fully understand Jacob Fugger's development into a modern, rationalistic, individualistic business man. Again, unless we remember the very special historical position which Augsburg, Fugger's native city, had enjoyed since the end of the fifteenth century, we shall not understand how Fugger, not only as merchant and financier, but also as mining entrepreneur, became a forerunner of the great captains of industry of the nineteenth and twentieth centuries. And finally, many a line in the portrait is properly illuminated only by an appreciation of the influence which played upon him from the immediate environment of his family, both his ancestors and his contemporaries.

Hence this study begins with a consideration of these factors which went so far toward determining the man and his work. To put it in other terms, Jacob Fugger received three inheritances, each of which we must appreciate before we can proceed to a consideration of what he accomplished with his inheritance.

German commercial history, in which the most striking and popular figure even today is that of Jacob Fugger, is marked by three brilliant epochs. The first of these falls within the Middle Ages; its scene is northern Germany and northern Europe in general. It is the period of the Hanseatic League, the period when the North German merchant plays the leading rôle in the trade of northern and eastern Europe, the period when the manufacture and even the public finance of the North European nations, including England, were strongly influenced by the Hanseatic merchants and capitalists.

When, toward the end of the fifteenth century, the Hanseatic League entered upon its decline, the center of German economic life moved from the north to the south. During the first two-thirds of the sixteenth century, the merchants of this region, the Fuggers early taking the lead, had a more influential share in the commercial, industrial, and financial life of Europe than ever before or since. Even among the Italians, the leading European merchants of the Middle Ages and the second commercial nation of the sixteenth century, unbiased judges conceded the leadership in European economic life to the South Germans during the middle of the sixteenth century. Lodovico Guicciardini, one-time Florentine merchant and later historian of the Netherlands, about 1560 admiringly called Anton Fugger, nephew and successor to Jacob in the control of the Fugger trading company, the king of European trade.

We may therefore call the Fugger period the second golden age in German commercial history. It ended during the last decades of the sixteenth century, when the supplies of precious metals brought from the New World robbed of their chief importance the European mines, which were controlled by the Germans; and when the state bankruptcies canceled most of the working capital of the German merchants. The final blow to the economic life of Germany was then dealt by the Thirty Years' War, which, together with the religious and political disunion of the German lands, brought on an economic decline so great that complete recovery came only after more than a century and a half had elapsed. Then, in the nineteenth and twentieth centuries, begins the third great period in German economic history, which gained momentum in the 1850's and 1870's and closed with the beginning of the World War in August, 1914.

The second of these periods of expansion, the Fugger epoch, may also be called the early capitalistic period. For, if one is justified in characterizing the late nineteenth and early twentieth centuries as the period of fully developed capitalism, we are equally correct in describing the late fifteenth and sixteenth centuries as the time when a vigorous capitalistic enterprise developed under the leadership of South German entrepreneurs. In this they were but carrying farther the work begun by Hanseatic merchants. During the fifteenth and sixteenth centuries, there spread rapidly through a fairly large and economically active class in Germany the capitalistic spirit—a consistent, unchecked, never-satisfied search after gain. This spirit found its most complete expression in the Augsburg of the sixteenth century. In this city, enormous capital accumulations (enormous, that is, according to the concepts and possibilities of the period) growing out of commerce and industry were being concentrated in the hands of a few large merchants. To meet the demands of this new spirit of enterprise, modern business forms and modern methods of organization were evolved in increasing numbers, even including great banking consortia, and commercial and industrial cartels—forms of capitalistic enterprise which have long been considered peculiar to the nineteenth and twentieth centuries.

Jacob Fugger is the chief embodiment of this early German capitalistic enterprise. Under his leadership, it spread from a few isolated individuals to a class (not a numerous one, to be sure) of outstanding business leaders. The rise of this new, powerful, and important social class is directly related to Fugger's activity. It is due to him that former efforts at creating a German entrepreneurship on a grand scale were at length crowned with success. Moreover, he represents a distinct type which became a model for successive generations; a type which in its ideology and its conduct, as well as in the example set in the organization and direction of economic life, was to be of the greatest significance for the further development of German entrepreneurship.

It would, however, be setting too narrow limits to the historical position of Jacob Fugger to view him only in his relation to German economic development. He was also a leading figure in European economic life, not only in the sense that his enterprises reached far beyond the boundaries of the Holy Roman Empire, and had an international scope, but even more in the sense that his achievements mark the culmination of early European capitalism, which had been developing in Italy since the beginning of the Renaissance.

Thus Jacob Fugger claims a place in European economic history, or, as the historians of our little planet sometimes say in a manner far from modest, in world economic history. His career marks the end of the medieval period and the opening of the modern. Among the business leaders of that period, among the rising mercantile class of Europe, this most important member of the Fugger family stands forth pre-eminent.

The translation into English is welcomed, since it serves to place this brief portrait study of the greatest of German merchants before a greatly widened circle of readers. This opportunity has been afforded me chiefly through the efforts of my colleague, Professor N. S. B. Gras, of the Graduate School of Business Administration of Harvard University; and I wish to express here my deep appreciation of his services in finding a publisher, and in supervising the translation and publication of the book.

My thanks are due also to Miss Mildred Hartsough, Associate in Research at the Graduate School of Business Administration, Harvard, for the preparation of the translation, as well as to my colleagues Geheimrat Oertel of Munich and Dr. Leidig for their friendly assistance in reading the translation.

TABLE OF CONTENTS

TABLE OF CONTENTS

ILLUSTRATIONS

CHAPTER I

THE ITALIAN INHERITANCE

THE development of the entrepreneurship of Jacob Fugger bears readily recognizable traces of that early European capitalism which arose in Renaissance Italy in contrast to the co-operative ideals of the medieval gilds. This is the starting point for the student who wishes to understand fully the forces that shaped the Augsburg merchant. By the "Italian Inheritance" is implied primarily a frame of mind, that spirit of rationalistic individualism which the Italians had developed earliest and most completely of all the European commercial nations and which also guided Jacob Fugger. It implies also (and this for Fugger as a European business leader was of considerable significance) the whole sum of practical models in business furnished by the Italian merchants ever since the time of the Crusades in the fields of exchange, wholesale trade, industry, colonial administration, and high finance. To what extent Jacob Fugger was in this respect indebted to the Italians can perhaps be most readily seen in the field of finance.

The earliest European bankers who achieved international financial importance were those of medieval Italy. This does not refer to the little, or even the more important, money-changers from Asti, Chieri, and similar Italian cities and towns, who, under the collective name of Lombards or Cahorsines, established their 'change counters in all the European trading cities of the Middle Ages, who on occasion did a pawn-broker's business like the Jews', and who sometimes even made loans to the spiritual and temporal princes. The reference is rather to those few large-scale Italian merchants and trading companies which from their head offices at home and from their branches placed themselves, as international financiers, at the service of the higher European aristocracy in its growing financial needs.

Numerous factors accounted for the early development of such a class of financiers in medieval Italy. One of the most important was the great expansion of Italian economic life, especially from the time of the Crusades. Out of this expansion, based especially on the trade with the Levant, arose two most important prerequisites for the development of Italian *haute finance*: sufficiently great accumulations of wealth and entrepreneurs competent to conduct international financial transactions.

Among the objective prerequisites, the environmental background which made possible the development of financiers in medieval Italy, the papal financial system must be given first place. The Roman Catholic Church had in the course of the Middle Ages become an international organization with a gigantic administrative system. The Papal See had partly involuntarily and partly on its own initiative risen to problems of important political policy, of the waging of war, and the like. For such a development, a carefully built-up system of papal taxation including all of Christendom early became indispensable. It was founded chiefly under Innocent III, about the beginning of the thirteenth century, on the basis of tithes, Crusade contributions, taxes imposed by the papal bureaucracy, and perquisites of all kinds, levied on all Christendom, but particularly on the clergy.

The Italian merchants, with their trading counters in all the great European centers, furnished ready and satisfactory instruments for the collection and transfer of all these dues. It was inevitable that these merchants should also supply loans to the pope in times of financial stress. Even more often, they performed this function for the upper ranks of clergy, who were not always in a position to pay the various levies demanded by Rome except by means of advances from the bankers. On the other hand, the

financiers who were connected with the papacy sometimes accepted deposits from the treasury of the
Papal See, when rich yields or an economical and able
administration had given rise to a surplus.

Though this connection with the papacy was the
chief basis for the early development of a class of
financiers in medieval Italy, other factors were also
favorable. An especially fruitful and certain field of
activity was opened to the financiers when the royal
lords began to develop their prerogative. Wherever
the overlord had important tariff immunities or other
trading privileges to grant, wherever he could grant
exemption from export duties on articles in which
trade on a large scale was possible, wherever the Crown
could distribute more or less monopolistic patents for
mining or for the salt industry, or for trade in the
products of these enterprises to those who had won
its favor, there the ground was prepared for the appearance and activity of the Italian financiers. On
their part, loans on a large scale were made in return
for economic privileges of the above-mentioned or
similar character. The practice became most common
in Italy itself, which during the course of the Middle
Ages became the richest and most active commercial
nation. Thus in the Kingdoms of Naples and Sicily
it was quite customary, even in the thirteenth century,
to finance and repay the large loans of the Florentine

and other bankers of central and northern Italy by granting them very profitable exemptions from export duties on grain shipped from Apulia, Calabria, etc., to Rome, Florence, and other points.

The relationship between Italian financiers and the English Crown developed on a similar basis of credit. The exemption from export duties on the fine English wool, which was the chief article of export in the Island and one of the most important articles in medieval international trade, constituted the most popular and satisfactory security by means of which the English kings for centuries obtained large loans from the powerful Italian bankers. The granting of similar privileges in the English tin-mining industry played a comparatively slight rôle. In France, the farming of coinage and taxation formed the chief bases on which the absolute monarchy likewise for centuries built up its great credits with Italian financiers. At times, as early as Philip the Fair, the Italians carried on almost the entire financial administration of the country as the mortgagees of important national revenues.

Most interesting of all, perhaps, are the changes in the rôles played by the different Italian cities in which the financial development took place that was to furnish a model for Jacob Fugger in the fifteenth century. In the twelfth and early thirteenth centuries, it was the inhabitants of various Lombard, Tuscan,. and other Italian cities who shared in the carrying of the most important international loans and thus began to lay the foundations of modern banking. From the late thirteenth and early fourteenth centuries, however, the Florentine bankers took over the leadership, in the Kingdom of Naples, in France, with the Papal See, and even in England. Under Edward III, the great Florentine trading companies of the Bardi and Peruzzi (who also played a predominant rôle as royal financiers in the Kingdom of Naples) for a time controlled almost the whole financial administration of England. The finest art of the financier—that of knowing when to give credit and when to refuse it—they seem, however, in the end to have lost. When they failed in 1345 in one of the most sensational bankruptcies in economic history, Edward III owed them enormous sums.

The importance of the Florentine financial world reached its culmination in the fifteenth century under the Medici, that family which may rightly be described by the title, often somewhat lightly accorded by history, of princely merchants. For several generations, from the first to the last quarter of the fifteenth century, the Medici had a determining influence in the finances of England, France, Naples (here especially with the other Florentine family of

Strozzi), and in an even greater degree in the finances of the papacy. Only after the death of Lorenzo de' Medici did other Tuscan bankers supplant this family in its relations with the Papal See. Among these were especially the Florentine Bindo Altoviti (whose immortality was assured even more securely by his self-sacrificing friendship with Raphael, Michelangelo, and Benvenuto Cellini than by his great mercantile achievements), and the Sienese Agostino Chigi, who as the Mæcenas of Italian Renaissance art has associated his name forever with one of the most brilliant epochs in the history of art.

It is shortly after the Medici disappeared from the European arena of financial activity that we first meet the Fuggers in relationships with the Papal See. From the end of the fifteenth century, these relations became much closer, reaching their height under Jacob Fugger in the first decades of the sixteenth century. For more than two decades, the great Augsburg merchant prince was the chief financial aid of the See in northern and eastern Europe.

In a later section of this book, where the various lines of Jacob Fugger's mercantile activity are traced, his financial operations will be discussed in more detail, especially those with the Papal See. Here it is sufficient to call attention to this branch of his activity by way of indicating the importance for the Augsburger of the Italian influence. It was indeed no merely superficial inheritance from the great Italian financiers which passed to Jacob Fugger when he took over the administration of the papal finances in eastern and northern Europe. The inner structure, the whole technique of the financial system, lay open to him as it had been brought to perfection by the Italians from the thirteenth century onward.

This borrowing from the Italian model was equally feasible with regard to the financial transactions of Jacob Fugger with the greatest temporal princes of his time. He was able to make use of their experiences and their business practices. Indeed, it was in part, as for example in the case of the great financial transactions with the Habsburgs, the same pledges and securities which had formerly served the Italians that Jacob Fugger now utilized. In the Kingdom of the two Sicilies only the dynasties had changed. The Spanish Habsburgs had taken the place of the Anjous; but the same rich revenues from the fruitful land remained, as well as the possibility of using them as security for loans. They were exploited by the new Spanish masters just as by the former Anjous; and the Fuggers came to the aid of the new masters just as the Italian merchants had to the old ones. The greater part of the loans which the German King, Ferdinand I, had to contract in the 1620's, in order to maintain the Habsburg position in eastern Europe, could no longer be secured by the resources of the Austrian inheritance; and Charles v was forced to secure the loans of his royal brother from Jacob Fugger by the pledge of his revenues from the South Italian possessions. Most of the loans of Ferdinand 1 which appear in the Fugger inventory of 1527 bear the inscription "referred to Naples"—*auf Neapel verwiesen.*

Conditions were not very different in Spain. There the incomes of the Grand Masters of the three religious knightly orders of Santiago, Alcántara, and Calatrava (to the latter, for instance, belonged the famous Almada quicksilver mines), represented an important source of revenue for the Spanish Crown after Ferdinand of Aragon had attached the Grand Mastership to the Crown. From the fifteenth century, it was customary to pledge with the merchants the incomes of these orders, as a whole or divided into fractions, as security for considerable advances of money; in the sixteenth century, this practice became much more common. Spanish capitalists competed in the business at first with the best-known Italian financiers of the late medieval and early modern period. Later Jacob Fugger, as in so many other branches of European finance, took the leadership from the Italians.

Italian influence on Jacob Fugger is marked not only in the fields of finance, but in various others of his many-sided interests. Outstanding examples to be cited are those of the wholesale spice trade and the trade in fine Italian silks. But perhaps the strongest of all the Italian influences was the intellectual, which permeated all his business activity. If the Augsburg mercantile genius finally outgrew his early model and became the chief exponent of economic rationalism and business capacity of his time, this was chiefly because of his own great initiative in developing the capitalistic spirit, his chief inheritance from Italy, to a degree hitherto unattained.

The story of the development of the capitalistic spirit in Europe is the story of the rise of the powerful individual, the outstanding personality in the field of material culture and of economic life. It was in Italy that the spirit of individualism developed out of the movement which we call the Renaissance; economic individualism also appeared first in Italy as one of the phenomena which characterized the modern world. In the realm of economic life as well as in religion, politics, and art, single outstanding individuals appeared in Italy, beginning about the eleventh century. They were men who wished to rise above their business contemporaries and who knew how to accomplish their aims, men who were not satisfied with the conventional methods of business procedure, which to be sure produced an income in keeping with their social position, but not much more. These were individuals who boldly conceived new business ideas, who understood how to turn to their own advantage the new opportunities offered by the increasing scale of operations.

What were the motives which led these men on to so feverish an activity? Was it the wish to rise higher in the social scale; was it ambition, lust for gold, desire for fame, the wish to further family interests? All these and other motives undoubtedly played a part, but the primary motive, especially with the most creative among them, was something else. In the background, often indeed in the subconscious, was the drive of strong creative individualism, the unceasing desire for activity which spurred them on in whatever field—which one was indeed more or less incidental—they found themselves. This need for the employment of his energies which constantly drove the individual on cannot be adequately explained, nor can it be resolved into its final elements. It is more than mere joy in achievement and power, more than habit, though all these are included. In the final analysis, it must be accepted as something inherent in all creative natures. It is expressed in classical form in the oft-quoted words of Jacob Fugger, its most important early German exponent. When a relative advised him to abandon an especially speculative part of his business, in order to enjoy in peace during the last years of his life the wealth that had been acquired with so much effort, Fugger replied that "he had no intention of so doing, that he wished to make a profit as long as he could." The reason is not told us, could not have been told us even by Jacob Fugger. The acquisition of wealth and of more wealth—not to be sure for wealth's sake alone—is implied in his remark to be an end in itself.

The external circumstances, the economic setting, had been favorable to the development and spread of the capitalistic spirit in Italy since the eleventh century. Better times had followed upon the difficult period of the ninth and tenth centuries, with their Saracen, Norman, and Magyar invasions, as well as other disturbances of economic life. The trade with Byzantium and the Levant, never entirely abandoned, could be taken up again on a larger scale. Then the Crusades brought the Italian merchants directly into the Greek-Arabian world, which they had formerly known only through the Byzantine market, and the mediation of the Byzantine traders. As a result of these events, numerous and inviting opportunities were open to the bolder and more enterprising spirits among the Italian merchants. The advantage was in fact a double one; not only were more profitable sources of supply opened, but buyers of Oriental goods appeared in Italy in increasing numbers from the eleventh century onward. A developing culture in Flanders, Germany, France, and England had widened the market, and the growing demand was naturally satisfied largely through the Italian cities.

Partly as cause and partly as effect of the increasing opportunities for economic enterprise, the spirit of economic individualism had sprung up in Italy since the twelfth century, especially among the more gifted of the merchants in the trading towns. Their property was growing; their credit and the deposits by relatives and by outsiders increased their financial strength. Everywhere there was confidence in these men of initiative; everywhere their credit was good. In addition to the class of powerful merchants which grew up, there was a group of bankers who were soon of international importance. A large part of the industry of the Orient was transplanted to Italy during the course of the Middle Ages. The Italian city states developed a colonial system in the Mediterranean, a system which was a precursor and a prototype for Spain and Portugal in the fifteenth and sixteenth centuries, and even for Holland in the seventeenth.

In the fields of government, of public administration, of diplomacy, and the conduct of war, the spirit of the Italian Renaissance gave rise to carefully reasoned-out systems; in the field of business enterprise, it resulted in economic rationalism. The former process is classically described in Jacob Burckhardt's *Kultur der Renaissance in Italien;* the simultaneous appearance of the latter he did not note, or at any rate did not comment upon. Yet the parallelism of the two developments, which sprang from one root, is patent. Renaissance rationalism shows itself in the farseeing, systematically thought-out trading practices, in the credit mechanism, in the organization of trading companies, and most of all, perhaps, in the introduction of double-entry bookkeeping. Parallel to the greatest creation of the Renaissance spirit —the state as a rational evolution—stands the economic system similarly conceived, the modern business undertaking, the capitalistic enterprise built up by individuals left to their own resources.

From Italy, capitalism spread throughout western Europe. This was partly the result of direct imitation, the merchants of these other countries apprenticing themselves, often in the literal sense of the word, to their Italian masters. In part, it was through the gradual development, throughout western Europe, of individualism which spread as a matter of course to the field of economic enterprise and, as the external conditions were favorable, found embodiment in isolated outstanding personalities.

Jacob Fugger's contact with the field of Italian enterprise came in his youth, when he laid the foundations, during his Venetian apprenticeship, of his later mercantile mastership. In Venice, and later in other Italian cities, the budding merchant saw daily with his own eyes how rapidly and surely the unwearying activities of powerful business men lifted them into the leading ranks of citizenship in the Italian city states, politically as well as socially. The Medici of Florence had begun as merchants the course of family development which was to culminate in princely rank. The history of other great mercantile families was analogous, if not quite so favored by fortune. Such examples must have fired the minds and the imaginations of the young sons of German merchants, while they remained in Italy as apprentices and later as representatives of their fathers' firms. This may well have given them those high aims in life which urged them on to the full exercise of their business acumen.

It is no accident that Jacob Fugger, long years after his return from Italy (as for example in the partnership agreement of the year 1494) still called himself Jacomo Fugger, that his brothers and business associates still called him by the Italian form of his

Christian name. The implicit inference is that he himself and his contemporaries thought of him as the bearer of the Italian inheritance.

To this example of the leading Italian business geniuses was added for Jacob Fugger the example of their intelligent management of business affairs, for which the Italians had perhaps a stronger psychological predilection than the Germans. Jacob Fugger had acquired in Italy precise knowledge of the most advanced mercantile practice, especially in bookkeeping, which enabled him later, on his frequent trips of examination, to test the accounts and balances of the various Fugger branches for himself, and— even more important—to have always at his command a detailed statement of the condition of the whole network of Fugger undertakings.

In this economic rationalism, expressed in an advanced system of keeping accounts, Jacob Fugger showed a strong touch of the modern; indeed, he ultimately reached a height in that essential of modern business which had been but rarely attained even in Italy. Matthäus Schwartz, later Fugger's valued chief bookkeeper, spent his years of apprenticeship in the Italian cities, where he eagerly sought, in Milan, Genoa, and Venice the best masters in his chosen profession. When he returned to Augsburg, he was engaged by Fugger, and soon found that he knew "little more than nothing" of the art of bookkeeping. The test undergone before his imposing new chief (he has preserved the scene in one of the pictures in his renowned *Kostümbiographie*) turned out badly for the young neophyte. He realized then, and more and more keenly during his work in the Augsburg office of the Fuggers, that he need not have sought so far afield what he could easily have learned at home as the apprentice of Jacob Fugger. To this extent had the former apprentice of the Italians become master in this important phase of his calling. We are of course concerned here not with the merely technical side of bookkeeping, but rather with its function and the purposes which it helped to achieve. What the Italian creators of bookkeeping—in the last analysis perhaps scarcely deliberately—tried to attain, and what made this creation of economic rationalism so indispensable in the training of the entrepreneur, was really a twofold function. In the first place, the entrepreneur was in a position, through accurate keeping of accounts, to ascertain clearly at any moment the exact condition of his business. Matthäus Schwartz, the pupil of Jacob Fugger, in his textbook on bookkeeping, shows his scorn and contempt for the merchants who think they can keep their accounts in their heads. "These little men write down their dealings in poorly kept scrap-books, or on slips of paper, stick them on the wall and make their reckonings on the window-sill." Such people could scarcely hope for business success. He who manages large enterprises must make use of the "wealth-creating art" of bookkeeping. It alone furnishes with complete security the most important prerequisites for business success. The enterprise must be reflected, Schwartz continues, in the bookkeeping as clearly as one's own face in the mirror. That is Jacob Fugger's own spirit wafted to us out of his countingroom.

More than all this, however, the proper keeping of accounts schools the capable business man in that objective capacity of seeing things as a whole as well as in detail. This function combined well with Fugger's own innate tendencies. The keen intellect which distinguished him always judged coolly and dispassionately the undertakings upon which he entered, especially in the case of speculations in money or goods. As exactly as with a pair of scales this man would weigh the possibilities and risks of an enterprise, or a business transaction. Nothing was concealed by a misplaced optimism, and everything was rejected which could not bear dispassionate, rational scrutiny. No measure of self-insurance was neglected. Only when all precautionary measures had been taken was the optimism so necessary to every entrepreneur justified. When we have studied the fixed determination with which Jacob Fugger denied unsecured credit to even the mightiest ruler of his time, when we have become familiar with the inflexible firmness of his requests for the payment of accounts, only then are we in a position fully to appreciate the cool rationalism of this man in business affairs. He held always to the maxim "en affaires comme en affaires," that is, business is business and must be so dealt with.

The guiding principles of this business genius are well illustrated in his relationship with the Emperors Maximilian I and Charles V. He attached himself with fidelity and conviction to the House of Habsburg, and so far as he could supported with the power of his wealth and his credit the imperial policy in both the temporal and the spiritual spheres. But never, so far as has been discovered, did Fugger allow the proud consciousness of his indispensability and his extraordinary power to be overwhelmed by all the flattery or all the pressure of the imperial officials and financial agents to the extent of neglecting cold and calm business calculations.[1] He granted credit only so far as was justified from a purely commercial point of view.

This attitude of coolly calculated objectivity toward all business ventures, which Jacob Fugger maintained during his whole lifetime, saved him from entering upon daringly speculative undertakings. It

[1] See Letters and Articles of Association, pp. 189 ff.

meant good fortune for him and for the development of the Fugger family partnership, for which Jacob Fugger laid the last foundation stones. A considerable number of important German and even Augsburg firms in the course of the sixteenth century fell victims to the search for large speculative monopoly profits. The Höchstetter of Augsburg failed in the 1620's after a brilliant mercantile career, which had brought them to the foremost rank of European business men. Their fall was the result of an attempt to accomplish what only the Rothschilds in the nineteenth century were able to carry through successfully, that is, to establish a world monopoly in quicksilver. Konrad Rott, another powerful Augsburg merchant in the second half of the sixteenth century, went bankrupt in the effort to create a world monopoly in the pepper trade with Portuguese India. Even Anton Fugger, nephew of Jacob and his successor in the direction of the Fugger enterprises, was led into an overly optimistic attempt, though one which promised large speculative profits, to create a central and eastern European monopoly in tin through the combination of the Bohemian and Saxon outputs. The attempt failed, costing the Fuggers not much less than a half million Rhenish gold gulden. An immense sum for those days, for in gold content it was equal to 4,000,000 gold marks. One must further take into account, in estimating the amount of the loss, the greater purchasing power of gold in the sixteenth century. No other German, indeed probably no other European trading house, would have been able to continue after such a setback. But Anton Fugger succeeded in stopping the losses in time. So strong was the foundation of the Fugger House, which Jacob Fugger had built up and which he was able to maintain so successfully largely because he gave his preference always to the smaller but more certain undertakings, rather than to the larger but more risky ones. He would never have considered a speculative misuse of the great capital resources which he controlled, such as we see on the part of the above-mentioned and various other Augsburg merchant princes of the sixteenth century. Here lies the key to the understanding of his unceasing and uninterrupted rise and his final success. It is as though this trader had studied and adopted the reasoning of Machiavelli, who despised mere pointless greed for power, and advised the true statesman to keep a cool head and seek only the attainable. The essential principles of Jacob Fugger's business conduct might well be similarly formulated. His is the same attitude which Friedrich von Gentz, a keen observer of human nature, noted at the beginning of the nineteenth century in the Rothschilds, and which he expressed in

the following words: It was characteristic of them
not to seek in any undertaking after excessive profit,
but to recognize the appropriate limits of each transaction. *Servare modum finemque tenere*—in this
maxim lies one of the chief secrets of their strength.
There is no doubt that with the means at their command they could have wrung greater profits out of
this or that single undertaking. But even though the
security of their enterprises would not have been
impaired, it was more profitable in the long run to
spread their energies over a greater variety of opportunities which recurred constantly, under all business conditions.

If we wish to sum up in one phrase the influence of
Italian economic rationalism on Jacob Fugger, we
might properly describe him as the most important
German product of the Renaissance in the realm of
economic life. It is proper to think of him as a creation of the Renaissance, not only because his business
activity so resembled that of the great Italians, but
also because in his private life the spirit of the Renaissance shows so strongly in his love of costly books
and manuscripts, and especially in the direction taken
by his artistic tastes. It was he who made the beginning of the Fugger library, which, greatly increased
by his nephews, Anton and especially Raimund, became famous throughout Europe and later, through

sale and gifts, formed important nuclei for the great libraries of Munich, Vienna, Heidelberg, Gran, and others. More than in his bibliophilistic tendencies, Jacob Fugger showed the Renaissance influence in his love of architecture. He was the first important German patron of art. In his Augsburg palace, and even more in his beautiful burial chapel of St. Anna in Augsburg, begun in 1510, he opened the way to the development of the early Renaissance movement in Germany. Just like the leading personalities of the Italian Renaissance, Fugger was moved by the desire to ensure the outward evidences of his lasting renown. Consequently, he constructed during his own lifetime this burial chapel at a very considerable outlay. The chapel served at the same time as a burial place and monument for his brothers, George and Ulrich, who had died before him. In 1518 occurred the dedication of the chapel, which forms the terminus for the central aisle of the Carmelite Church of St. Anna to the West. Its beautifully proportioned interior glittered with marble, colors, and gold. The architect who labored here with such success is unknown, but we do know, through the researches of Philipp Maria Halm, of the artist who introduced his masterpieces into the structure designed by this unknown architect. Jacob Fugger secured in Adolf Daucher a talented sculptor for the great epitaph relief on the broad rear wall of the chapel, for the lovely figures in wood on the choir-stalls, for the charming cherubim of the chancel, and, above all, for the masterpiece of the chapel, the altar with its deeply moving vesper picture. Like his patron, Daucher had subjected himself to the spirit of the Italian Renaissance, and thereby to the spirit of classical antiquity. Humanism, which had stirred the minds of the Augsburg scholars of the Fugger circle, such as Dr. Konrad Peutinger, Dr. Othmar Nachtigall, and others, had also affected the Augsburg artists. The first evidences, found in this Fugger chapel of St. Anna, are of considerable significance for the development of German art. Therein lies, too, its chief charm as the product of Fugger's love of art and his patronage. Hence the importance of the recent artistic restoration of this chapel, which was due chiefly to the keen interest of Prince Karl Ernst Fugger-Glött, and to the expert direction of the work of restoration by Philipp Maria Halm.

On the cleaned marble of the choir-screen, the writer found inscriptions scratched by travelers of the 1620's. Even at that time, the chapel must have been widely visited, not only by the leading personalities of the day and by personal acquaintances of the House of Fugger, but also by the general art-loving public, which appreciated the achievements both of the German mercantile genius and of the great German artist. Since then, millions of Germans and foreigners have sought out this beautiful chapel erected by Fugger out of gratitude for his business success and as a monument to his enduring fame.

Not only the crypt itself of the German merchant is in the Renaissance style; the text of his epitaph was likewise conceived in the same spirit. In it comes unconcealed to expression the justifiable self-satisfaction of a great man, who recognized posthumous renown as one of the great motive forces behind the activity of modern man. Freely translated, it runs thus:

To God, All-Powerful and Good

Jacob Fugger of Augsburg, ornament to his class and to his country, Imperial Councilor under Maximilian I and Charles V, second to none in the acquisition of extraordinary wealth, in liberality, in purity of life, and in greatness of soul, as he was comparable to none in life, so after death is not to be numbered among the mortal.

CHAPTER II

THE INFLUENCE OF AUGSBURG

G REAT was the influence of Italy, as we have seen, of the Italian business man, and of the development of economic rationalism in the Italian Renaissance upon Jacob Fugger. But these factors alone cannot explain the rise and activity of this business leader. This is shown by the fact that the Augsburg merchant developed lines of economic enterprise which were scarcely known to the Italians. An outstanding example is found in the extractive industry, both mining and smelting. Jacob Fugger attained a position in this field which made him an undisputed leader in Europe; and he became the forerunner of the German captains of industry of the nineteenth and twentieth centuries. In this phase of his activity he followed in the footsteps, not of the Italian, but of the German, and particularly of the Augsburg, entrepreneurs. Here, as in other phases of his business life, the roots of Jacob Fugger's activity lie in the special economic rôle played by Augsburg, his native city, during the late fifteenth and early sixteenth centuries, that is to say, during his lifetime.

The dependence, to be sure, was mutual, for Jacob Fugger helped to shape the business life of the Augsburg of his and of succeeding generations, more than any other citizen of the old imperial city ever did. The Augsburg of the Renaissance, standing great and imposing at the entrance to the modern period, is not merely by accident the scene of Jacob Fugger's life-work, not merely the outward frame of his existence; it is to a considerable extent in its new economic framework the product of his labors. Fugger broke many of the paths, especially in the field of economic organization, followed during his own lifetime and long afterward by other Augsburg entrepreneurs. Much even in the present economic structure of the city may be recognized by the historically minded as the outgrowth of seeds which, if not planted by Jacob Fugger, were at least nurtured by him to an early maturity which lasted over into a much later period.

But, however strongly this genius impressed on the economic life of Augsburg the stamp of his own personality, his own development was to an equal degree influenced and conditioned by the setting furnished by his native city. In Lübeck, in Cologne, or even in Ulm or Nuremberg, Fugger would never have become what he finally did become. In none of these other German economic centers at the end of the Middle Ages and the beginning of the modern period could he have become, to name only one phase of his activity, the greatest industrial magnate of his time. In Augsburg, the mercantile talent was favored by geographical position and by the foundations laid by its other enterprising citizens.

Rarely had a city of the Middle Ages (especially in what was for that conservative time so short a period as fifty years) experienced so complete a transformation of its economic structure as had Augsburg at just this time. When Jacob Fugger was born, on March 6, 1459, Augsburg was by no means the important center of German material culture which it had become by 1525, when the last pages were written in the diary of that most famous of its sons. Up to the middle of the fifteenth century, the old *Augusta Vindelicorum* was outranked in economic importance by the South German cities, at least by Vienna and Nuremberg, to say nothing of the North German, especially the Hansa, cities.

None of the Augsburg trading companies—not even Meuting, which during that period was the leading firm—could be compared with the "great Ravensburg Company." Built up by able business men of Ravensburg, Constance, and other imperial cities of the Lake Constance region, and later by merchants from St. Gall, Berne, Freiburg in Switzerland, Nuremberg, and perhaps even Frankfurt on the Main, this powerful trading company maintained its leadership of South German trade from the second half of the fourteenth century until 1480. Even in the next generation, the financial strength of the Ravensburg Company was not equaled by any in Augsburg. Its working capital of about 140,000 gold gulden was exceeded by the Fugger trading company only in the second decade of the sixteenth century. From that time on, the Ravensburg Company was overtaken by other Augsburg trading groups as well. By the late fifteenth century the leadership in activity and in economic energy had passed to the Augsburg merchants.

During the first decades of the sixteenth century, this city on the Lech rose with extraordinary rapidity to the uncontested leadership of South German, indeed of all German, economic life. Something of an impression, at least of a quantitative character, of this development can be secured from the tax records of the old imperial city, which fortunately have been preserved down to the present day. From this reliable source, it is possible to see with all certainty how in the last decades of the fifteenth and first of the sixteenth centuries the larger fortunes in Augsburg increased in both size and number. In 1467 only 39 citizens of Augsburg had property to an amount which in 1509 could be claimed by 122, and in 1540 by 278 individuals. And while in 1467 the sum of the property of these 39 wealthy citizens amounted to between 230,000 and 460,000 gold gulden, in 1509 the 122 reached a total figure of between 1,300,000 and 2,600,000, and in 1540 the 278 claimed between 5,000,000 and 10,000,000. These figures, furthermore, since they represent tax declarations, are minima rather than maxima. It is probable that the total taxable property of Augsburg citizens quadrupled between 1470 and the end of the century; and by 1550, it must have been thirteen times as great as in 1470.

Abroad and at home, the reputation of Augsburg for wealth and for the financial strength of its citizens spread almost like a fable. Whenever money was needed in the contemporary world, loans were sought in Augsburg; and the source seemed inexhaustible. Martin Luther expressed the general opinion when in one of his "table talks" he remarked that "Augsburg could produce thirty tons of gold in three weeks, which was more than the Kaiser could do."

The writer has elsewhere [1] noted that the majority of these fortunes, on the basis of which the new Augsburg arose, were built up fundamentally in trade. Not trade at random, but a trade which in connection with the rising Augsburg manufacture, especially that

[1] *Zur Genesis des modernen Kapitalismus, Forschungen zur Entstehung der grossen bürgerlichen Kapitalvermögen am Ausgang des Mittelalters und zu Beginn der Neuzeit, zunächst in Augsburg* (Leipzig, 1904).

of fustian weaving, was developing large proportions. A large number of Augsburg families owed their rise to a position of economic prominence to the union of fustian weaving and trade. It was not only the Fugger family which moved from the weavers' craft into the gild of merchants, and from that into a position of commercial leadership in Europe. Alongside them can be placed the Ehem, the Bimmel, the Höchstetter, and others. Their ancestors had stood at the loom; their descendants were merchants of world-wide fame and the bankers of kings and princes. Today, their names are known only to the research student and to local town history; but in the sixteenth century they were recognized internationally in the market and on the exchange.

A considerable number of these Augsburg families developed their fortunes to imposing proportions during the course of several generations. The underlying factors may be briefly traced. Augsburg merchants— especially under the leadership of Jacob Fugger—concentrated more and more during this period on mining and the trade in ore. In so doing, they were much more successful than even the merchants of Nuremberg and Leipzig in drawing into their coffers a large proportion of the great profits to be made in this period of transition from the Middle Ages to the modern period, profits in the mines and smelting works and the metal trade of the Holy Roman Empire and other European countries.

During this period, mining and the ore trade were undoubtedly the leading economic interests of the Holy Roman Empire, aside of course from agriculture. It was not an overstatement when Charles v in a mandate of the year 1525—the year of Jacob Fugger's death—referred to the mines as the greatest gift and source of profit "which Almighty God had vouchsafed the German lands." Neither was it an exaggeration when he estimated the yearly production of the mines of the Holy Roman Empire at a minimum of 2,000,000 gold gulden. And Charles chose too low rather than too high a figure when, in the above-mentioned mandate, he reckoned the inhabitants of the Holy Roman Empire employed in mining and smelting at 100,000. For comparison (although it must be remembered that the figure cited by Charles v was only an estimate), it may be noted that in 1882 German manufacturing statistics listed only 430,000 employed in mining, smelting, and salt manufacturing. And this in spite of the expansion in the German mining industry during the 1870's.

During the fifteenth and early sixteenth centuries, mining developed rapidly in the Holy Roman Empire, giving Germany an economic advantage over other European countries. The fact that Augsburg

profited especially from this development was the result of several factors. There was, first, its favorable
geographical situation with reference to the mineral
resources of the Tyrol, which was at its height between
1500 and 1530. There was, in addition, the mercantile capacity of its citizens, and the special favor of
Maximilian I, the lord of the Tyrol. Maximilian's en-
thusiasm for Augsburg had, to be sure, a background
at least partly materialistic, in so far as that imprac-
tical romanticist, ever in debt, could always find here
the necessary funds for his great expenditures on administration, war, and luxury.

The profits of the Augsburg merchants in mining
and trade in the products of the mine reach, for the
fifteenth and sixteenth centuries, into the millions of
gold gulden. Trade in ore was the primary interest of
the leading merchants of the city. In the case of a
number of the Augsburg trading companies of the
period, it may be seen, as their sphere of activity
widens and their importance increases, how other
articles of trade decline in importance in comparison
with ore and metals. Perhaps later, when research has
been pushed further, this will be seen to have been a
characteristic course of development for the period;
as yet, it can only be pointed out as of frequent oc-
currence.

The prominence of metals as articles of trade for the

great Augsburg trading companies was due in large part to the relationship between these companies and the imperial financial agents or princes. Governments, especially that of the ever needy Habsburgs, looked upon the mineral resources of their territories (the Tyrol, Hungary, Bohemia, etc.), over which they had one form or another of control, as the best security for financial advances. In this way, the big Augsburg trading companies were led into the metal trade simultaneously with the lending business, and often earned as large sums in the one as in the other. The individual merchant often rose from metal trading on a small scale to large-scale operations by means of loans to "ore-wealthy" princes. From wholesale trade in metals it was only a step to the acquisition of mines, mining stocks, smelting works, and thus to entrance into the mining industry.

In the case of the clear-minded Augsburg merchants, this step was not always taken voluntarily; in general, they did not enter eagerly upon the risks of mining enterprise. They found the trade in the products more congenial than the risks of the industry, with the threat of stock assessments, and the heavy investment in fixed capital. Unless there was an urgent necessity which led them into the earlier stages of production, they preferred to remain buyers of the end products, with larger and relatively certain profits, while others bore the greater risks.

Not that they entirely avoided risks. At this time, there was rarely a direct business relationship between the mining entrepreneur and the merchant, in which the latter did not undertake to furnish a considerable part of the capital and thus to share the risks of the producer. The merchant of the medieval and early modern period was called upon here, as in other branches of industry, to perform a function which later—though only toward the middle of the nineteenth century—was taken over by the financiers and banking houses. At this early period, the merchant was the only agency through which the industrial entrepreneur could get the capital which he needed for the expansion of his business. Even though he did not carry on mining himself as the owner or operator of mines or as stockholder, the metal trader of the fifteenth and sixteenth centuries often had to invest considerable sums in mining.

That might take place in any of several ways. Sometimes the merchant had to make advances to the smaller mine operators whose products he bought. In other cases the products as they were purchased from the mine were not yet in salable form, and the merchant who carried on business on a large scale had to set up smelting works where the crude ore could be refined to a merchantable form. Either of these practices, especially in view of the great expansion of the mining industry in the first decades of the sixteenth century, often required large sums of money. A considerable proportion of the wealth of Augsburg was thus profitably invested—invested in channels more valuable socially than that other fraction (perhaps not much smaller) which disappeared in the Danaides sieve of princely loans.

But there was an even more important cause for the investment of South German and especially Augsburg commercial capital in the mining industry than the financial needs of the mine owners. That was the financial need of the government. The metal trade and the loans to territorial princes came to form a closed economic circle into which all those merchants must inevitably penetrate who wished to carry on this most distinguished branch of business. The territorial prince as sovereign was in a position to take up or buy up from the mine operators—at a price lower than the market price, naturally—the whole mining production of his lands. And frequent recourse was had to this right; and the way in which it was carried out, so as to relieve state finances, was of considerable significance for the development of Augsburg entrepreneurship in the sixteenth century. Naturally the prince did not take over into his own administration the various monopolies in mining which were in his control. That would have required operating capital which he did not possess. Rather, he exploited his monopolies through the merchants, selling them to the highest bidder, who undertook in addition to pay immediately to the prince at least a large part of those profits which would normally have been drawn out over a period of years. In addition, preference was given to those entrepreneurs who showed themselves most agreeable to the prince in his financial necessities by granting further loans.

In the terminology of the time, the monopolies which the financial needs of the princes thus created for the great entrepreneurs were called deals (*Käufe*) or contracts, and references were common to copper, tin, or silver deals, and to ore contracts. These ore contracts were, at times, and so long as the conditions remained favorable in the particular branch concerned, among the most profitable lines of business known to the sixteenth century. To be sure, they often had a strongly speculative aspect, especially when a single entrepreneur undertook by means of them to establish an absolute monopoly over a more or less extended area. Then they involved a large element of risk. A tendency in this direction was particularly marked in Augsburg in the sixteenth century. But so long as the desire for monopolies did not over-reach itself, these ore contracts were a relatively certain and profitable business, and naturally attracted the attention of the richest merchants. In the sixteenth century one great Augsburg firm after another entered this field.

The needy princes, and especially the extraordinarily skilled financial agents and councilors of the Habsburgs, knew how to stimulate this interest artificially; and often long before the expiration of such a contract they had offered it on monopolistic terms to each of several of the newer members of the Augsburg mercantile circle. A deliberately fostered competition ensued, which was to the interest of imperial finances; for playing one competitor against another naturally contributed most to the royal treasury. The result with regard to the development of entrepreneurship in Augsburg was the rise of a new type of business leader out of a class that was very strong financially though not numerically. These men, who appeared in Nuremberg, Leipzig, and other cities, but especially in Augsburg, were no longer strictly merchants, and they were not yet strictly industrialists in the present sense of the word. Directly, they had little to do with the production of ores and metals; indirectly, they had a great deal. Primarily, they financed production and directed it. They took charge of the market throughout the world. They were the putting-out entrepreneurs for the smaller mine operators. Without their help, mining, so soon as costly investments were necessary, would have come to a standstill, the employees being thrown out of work, and the invested capital lost.

Jacob Fugger became the prototype of this class of business leader. In the Fugger undertakings, the other lines of business gradually declined (as regards profits at any rate), even the big financing operations, in favor of the direct and indirect acquisition and sale of mining products. At the end of his life, Jacob Fugger could be appropriately described as an industrial entrepreneur, although important remnants of his commercial interests still clung to him.

It is in just this aspect that Fugger was of the greatest significance for German economic development. In the flourishing mining industry, both within the Holy Roman Empire and elsewhere which he controlled, he was faced by problems heretofore unknown. He was led into technical problems of mining and smelting, and had to invest his capital in their solution, just as have the industrial captains of the Rhine and Upper Silesia since the beginning of the nineteenth century. But the chief problem for Fugger. was that of organizing and regulating mining production and the trade in the products of the mine on a scale corresponding to the needs of contemporary economic life.

In the development of this aspect of the Fugger business, the Augsburg setting was of decisive importance. For here, and in South Germany generally, predecessors and contemporaries helped to show Fugger the way. This was the case in Silesia, where Jacob Fugger succeeded in taking over the greater part of the Reichenstein gold mining, following the attempts in this field of other German trading houses, especially the Augsburg Welser-Vöhlin House, and the Grander trading company, also of Augsburg. This was also the case in the Tyrol, the most important mining district of the fifteenth and sixteenth centuries. So far as can be ascertained, the Augsburg trading company of Ludwig Meuting was the first— aside from smaller Viennese predecessors—to enter on a large scale the Habsburg mining field by means of "silver contracts." Its first large contract in this field was taken over in 1456. At that time, the Meuting trading company loaned Duke Sigmund of the Tyrol, who belonged to the House of Habsburg, 35,000 gulden for the purchase of silver from the miners and smelters. In return, all the silver produced at Schwaz, Gossensass, and elsewhere in the Duchy of the Tyrol was to be turned over to the Meuting trading house exclusively at the price of 7¾ Rhenish gold gulden per silver mark (two-thirds of a pound), until the debt had been completely repaid. The House of Meuting began with this Tyrol contract the development of a field of business which Jacob Fugger was later to exploit with signal success through the combination of a trading, industrial, and financial undertaking.

The relation of the Fugger House to its mercantile and industrial competitors in Augsburg soon changed. After Jacob Fugger had taken over the leadership of the business, the pupil of Meuting and of other ore traders soon became the master. The recipient became a contributor to the economic development of his native city. Following the example of Jacob Fugger and his business methods, one great Augsburg trading company after another, rising with and after the Fugger House, entered the mining field. Fugger repaid a hundredfold what he had taken over from his Augsburg and other South German predecessors.

In other lines of business as well as the mining industry, predecessors of Jacob Fugger were pathfinders for him, only to have him later surpass them. There is a long list of Augsburg business men who developed the Swabian fustian industry into a stepping stone upon which Jacob Fugger's ancestors themselves began the ascent to greatness, and upon which even Jacob rested at the beginning. Other branches of trade might be mentioned, such as the trade in spices, silks, and other goods from Italy, especially from Venice, in which Fugger followed the footsteps of many forerunners in his native city. Indeed, we find with Fugger, as with so many great men, that their originality lies not in the discovery of new fields of enterprise, but in the way in which they develop to the fullest extent the possibilities created by their predecessors.

This was particularly true in the case of the financing business, the most important of Fugger's many activities. Though the Italians were here the greatest models, Fugger found also in his South German environment a few merchants who had entered upon this business. From the researches of Aloys Schulte,[1] it is not certain whether the Welser-Vöhlin firm, which united entrepreneurs from Memmingen and Augsburg, preceded the Fuggers in financial relationships with the popes. It seems at least not improbable. At any rate, by the middle of the fifteenth century the Nuremberg merchant, Konrad Baumgartner (1380–1464), had established business connections with the Papal See.

This same following of a precedent appears in Fugger's relations to the temporal princes, the Habsburgs. Long before Fugger had built up that intimate business relationship with Maximilian I, which often alone

---

[1] *Die Fugger in Rom. 1495–1523*, 2 vols. (Leipzig, 1904).

enabled the Emperor to carry out his ambitious political plans, other Augsburg merchants had granted credit to the Habsburg rulers. Reference has already been made to the Ludwig Meuting Company, which loaned sums running up into the tens of thousands of Rhenish gulden to the Habsburg, Sigmund of the Tyrol. Maximilian I, German Emperor and successor to Sigmund in the control of the ore-rich Tyrol, also secured loans from other Augsburg merchants, as for instance the Gossembrot, even before he did from Fugger. It was these business connections which brought Maximilian I into closer and closer touch with the old imperial city, not only materially but intellectually as well. Thus was prepared for our Jacob Fugger the way to high finance with the Habsburgs. It was left to him not only to carry on boldly and at the same time cautiously these established business connections, but to extend them also into the political field, as will be pointed out later.

In addition to the business spirit of his fellow citizens, the whole economic policy of the local environment is significant for the development of business genius. What the entrepreneur needs first of all for the full play of his capacity is economic freedom. The policy of leaving the individual free to pursue his own economic interests as the basic economic policy of the state was born of the eighteenth-century Anglo-

French liberal philosophy and given its clearest literary expression by Adam Smith. It did not win general acceptance, however, until the nineteenth century. The towns, the princes, and most of society in the sixteenth century thought quite differently on this subject. The minds of men were still dominated by an ideal of Christian co-operation, rather than by one of economic individualism. The medieval system of economic ethics, formulated in the thirteenth century by Saint Thomas Aquinas, and in theory at least predominant until well into the eighteenth century, rested entirely upon the prohibition of the unrestrained pursuit of profit, and upon the prohibition of free competition, and a price policy dictated by the interests of the entrepreneur alone. At the basis of the medieval economic philosophy was the idea of a sufficient livelihood, the theory that the individual should strive for an income appropriate to his class, but not for much more.

The medieval town and the medieval state tried to carry out this economico-ethical system by means of gild regulation. The gild principle operated against too great an extension of the business of the individual entrepreneur. The general attitude is expressed in the saying: What can nourish two should not be absorbed by one. The gild principle was also, in the interest of the consumers, opposed to any attempt at a monopolistic price policy. Prices should be governed, not by private interest, but by justice. So taught the Schoolmen, and so even in the sixteenth century taught Luther when he laid down the principle in his great "Treatise on Trade and Usury:" "It is not right to say 'I will sell my wares as dear as I can or desire,' but 'I will sell my wares as dear as I should, or as is right and proper.' " The anticapitalistic tendency of the Middle Ages reaches its clearest expression in the canonical prohibition of usury, which placed an obstacle in the way of all extension of credit.

The attempt to draw the whole economic life of the medieval towns into the philosophy of the gild system was, however, only partly successful. There is no doubt that even in his own time, in Italy especially, the economic ideal of Saint Thomas Aquinas was in crass contrast with reality in the more important commercial centers. The great merchants of Venice, Genoa, and other cities were by no means satisfied with an income merely appropriate to their class. As far as they were concerned, the capitalistic spirit described above had long since overcome the gild limitations on the acquisition of profits. The situation was similar in the other economically advanced countries and towns of western and central Europe.

The author has in his *Studien zur Geschichte*

kapitalistischer Organizationsformen and in an essay
which appeared in 1925 in *Schmoller's Jahrbuch* en-
titled *Die Finanznot des Staates und die Genesis des
europäischen Unternehmertums* indicated that it was
the growing financial needs of the Church and the
state which forced these two powers to protect the
merchants when they, in opposition to the precepts
of Christian doctrine and against the views of the
greater part of the society of the Middle Ages and the
sixteenth century, gave free play to their desire for
the acquisition of profits. Church and state could no
longer, even in the fourteenth century, dispense with
the profit-making merchant. Their own needs, and
the greatly increased monetary demands of the
"grosse Politik," as well as of administration and of
the conduct of war, were too great for that. These
two greatest powers of public life were thus forced
through their financial straits to call for help on the
capitalistic merchant, to avail themselves of his services and thus greatly to increase his significance and
his influence.

The commercial policy of the great German trading centers had also by Jacob Fugger's time developed
to a point where it more or less tolerated the capitalistic spirit of the leading merchants. This was not true
in all cases. Among the South German cities, Basel
held out most strongly against the modern spirit and

the new economic ideals. There the petty bourgeoisie strongly opposed a group of merchants who in the second half of the fifteenth century showed their acceptance of the profit-making ideal in their founding of trading companies and in their monopolistic tendencies. Victory went to the former. With the aid of the political forces, which set up the gilds in Basel, an economic policy was carried into effect which strongly favored handicraft and the middle class, while it almost completely shut out the great trading companies. The gild ideal prevailed over the concept of freedom of the individual in the pursuit of his economic interests.

Augsburg in Jacob Fugger's time furnished a direct contrast to Basel. From Augsburg, and especially from the House of Fugger, was launched the request to Dr. Eck that he come out in his famous disputations in defence of an interest rate of five per cent. Augsburg may be considered the most progressive German town of the time in her business ethics and economic policy. She took an outstanding position in the great social and economic struggles of the sixteenth century, which played themselves out chiefly in the legislative bodies, both local and national, but which were waged about the pulpits and university chairs of the contemporary moral theologians as well. Economic liberalism and individualism pre-

vailed in the Council of the imperial city. Her neigh-
bors, the imperial cities around Lake Constance and
in the Allgäu, under the leadership of Ravensburg,
the headquarters of the Ravensburg Company, at a
joint meeting demanded that the working capital of
a trading company should not exceed 100,000 gold
gulden; the Councils of Nuremberg and Ulm even
wished to set the maximum figure at 25,000 gold
gulden. Augsburg alone supported the capitalistic
group unreservedly. Its Council demanded that no
limits should be set to the internal or external extension of the trading companies.

The exponent of the new economic temper of
Augsburg, the defendant of the Renaissance spirit in
the mercantile circles of Augsburg, was the Human-
ist, Dr. Konrad Peutinger. This was the same man to
whom Jacob Fugger went for counsel in all the juristic
and canonical problems of his profession and his business. Peutinger, more than any other, worked for the
freedom of trading companies, for freedom in the
making of prices, and for the toleration of capitalistic
monopolies and cartels. His attitude, in direct opposition to medieval economic ethics in the question
of price formation, for example, is clearly expressed
in the following sentences: "Every merchant is free
to sell his wares as dear as he can and chooses. In so
doing, he does not sin against canonical law; neither

is he guilty of antisocial conduct. For it happens often enough that merchants, to their injury, are forced to sell their wares cheaper than they bought them."

By a number of brilliant essays expressing his opinion on trade legislation and by the drafting of several very progressive trading laws for Charles v, Peutinger created a place in imperial policy and imperial legislation for the new economic philosophy which had found its clearest and most practical expression in Augsburg. This took place as the result of the closest co-operation between the jurist Peutinger and Jacob Fugger, the practical business man. It would be hard today to say which of the two was the intellectual leader and which the follower. Apparently we have here two minds attuned alike: the modern jurist who, in the spirit of the Roman law, in the spirit of a pagan individualism, turned his back on the essential principle of the German-Christian social organization (solidarity); the other, a modern merchant, who would not tolerate the setting of limits in the interests of altruism to his desire for the acquisition of profits, and to his outstanding entrepreneurship. Under the philosophical leadership of Dr. Peutinger, and the pressure of the growing number of big entrepreneurs, among which the Fuggers from the beginning of the sixteenth century played an ever more commanding rôle, the Augsburg Council came out for the complete freedom of its entrepreneurs from any restraint.

It was only in such an atmosphere that Jacob Fugger could have played the part that he did, not only on behalf of his family and his native city, but on behalf of the economic life of all Europe. It was because Augsburg in some measure anticipated the philosophy of economic individualism which reached its maturity only in the nineteenth century that Jacob Fugger was able to take on, at least in outline, the character of a modern entrepreneur.

CHAPTER III

THE FAMILY

THE present time is characterized by such a rapid tempo of economic development that the work of a single generation often suffices to bring an enterprise into a commanding position. Stories are current of business men, especially in the United States of America and Australia, who from nothing rise in one generation to become millionaires and the directors of huge undertakings. In earlier times, with the limited possibilities for the accumulation and concentration of capital, and with a much slower business pace, it required several generations to win a position of business leadership. And if the first able generation was not followed by an equally strong second and third, then the rise to greatness of the first order was not achieved.

It is therefore of some value to study the generations of the Fugger family which preceded Jacob, in order to see what he inherited from them. The founder of this most famous of German commercial families came in the second half of the fourteenth

century from the village of Graben on the Lechfeld
to settle in Augsburg. Unrestrained fantasy has built
up various legends around the dim figure of this
ancestor of the House of Fugger. In the light of critical investigation it appears that Hans Fugger was
probably one of those country weavers who had been
for centuries so common in the Swabian villages, and
who worked under the domestic system for the ex-
porting Augsburg merchant. He was apparently energetic and ambitious and became convinced that he
stood a better chance of advancing economically in
Augsburg than in his little village; and so about 1380
he moved into the city.

At first Hans Fugger was probably only a weaver,
but the expansion of fustian weaving in South Germany offered an opening for mercantile enterprise.
While many of his fellow craftsmen in town and
country became more and more dependent upon the
enterprising Augsburg merchants, who controlled
the import of the raw cotton through Venice and
the export of the finished cloth, Hans Fugger rose
to the rank of merchant himself. He began to import
the cotton and sell his own fustian in return, and
gradually that of other less enterprising craftsmen as
well. Soon he seems to have dealt in other wares that
figured in the German-Italian trade. It is certain
that his two sons Andreas and Jacob I did so; and

Andreas is said to have been officially enrolled in the gild of merchants. Some sources indicate that it was only the next generation which took this step. In any case, Jacob remained a highly respected member of the weavers' gild, although even with him trading interests certainly exceeded those of the craft.

Until the middle of the fifteenth century, the brothers carried on together the business inherited from their father. Then came the separation. Andreas and his line, known as the "Roe" Fuggers from the coat of arms which they adopted in 1462, at first took a more prominent position than Jacob's branch, that of the "Lily." But not for long; the sons of Andreas went bankrupt, and from henceforth the name of the "Roe" Fuggers disappeared from the mercantile annals of Augsburg.

Meanwhile the Fuggers of the Lily rose slowly but uninterruptedly in the course of three generations to a position of European renown. It was this branch which possessed the indispensable prerequisite of marked business capacity through successive generations. Jacob I died in 1469, while most of his children were still small; but his capable widow, the daughter of Franz Bäsinger, master of the mint and merchant, guided the enterprise with a sure hand through the dangerous waters of the transition to the next generation—that passage which brought disaster to so many merchant families. With the help of her oldest son, Ulrich, born in 1441, and later with the aid of his two brothers, George and Jacob II, the courageous woman was able not only to preserve the Fugger fortune but actually to increase it. She carried on the business energetically and successfully until her sons were able to free her entirely from a responsibility so unusual for a woman.

The Widow Fugger had borne seven sons, but all except Ulrich, George, and Jacob II, later known as "the Rich," died as children. Jacob II had already taken first orders and was prebendary in Herrieden (in middle Franconia); but in 1478, in order to make the continuance of the business as certain as possible, he abandoned his profession. Thus did the theologian become a merchant. A similar transformation occurred about three hundred years later when that other bright star of German economic history, Maier Amschel Rothschild, whom his family intended for a rabbi, became instead the founder of a financial dynasty.

Just how much Jacob Fugger the Rich owed to the preparations and to the example of his two older brothers, Ulrich (born in 1441) and George (born in 1453), it would be difficult to establish now with any exactness. It is certain that they were clever merchants who increased the Fugger fortune and car-

Birthplace of Jacob Fugger in Augsburg;
the First House in Foreground

ried on the sound business traditions of their forefathers. Ulrich, the elder, seems to have exceeded his
younger brother, who became the founder of the
two Fugger lines which are flourishing today (those
of Raimund and Anton), not only in business experience—which was natural in view of his advantage
in years—but also in mercantile capacity. In any case,
Ulrich directed the business, as the leader of the common enterprise, until his place was taken by Jacob,
the youngest of the brothers. His talent would undoubtedly stand out more brightly in the chronicles
of the House of Fugger were it not so overshadowed
by the genius of Jacob.

It must by no means be forgotten that much of
what was brought to full fruition by Jacob had
previously been begun by Ulrich with the assistance
of George. Thus it was Ulrich who began the fateful
business connection between the Fuggers and the
House of Habsburg. The old chronicle of the Fugger
family, which goes back to the sixteenth century,
describes as follows how the Fuggers became court
purveyors to the German kings and emperors: "It
was in the year 1473, when Emperor Frederick III.
was in Augsburg and with Prince Maximilian (later
Emperor Maximilian I) prepared to go to Trier to
the Imperial Diet, that this Ulrich Fugger began the
first business dealings with the Austrian archdukes,

dealings which from that time onward increased constantly. He supplied the Emperor with silk and woollen cloth upon the journey, and received from His Imperial Majesty the Fugger coat of arms with the lilacs."

It was the older brothers, also, who developed the wide geographical range of the Fugger business relationships. Long before Jacob became the dominant influence in the enterprise, its connections reached from Italy in the south to the Netherlands in the north, and to Silesia, Poland, and Hungary in the east. The same may be said with regard to the scope of the business. Ulrich seems to have greatly extended the old Fugger commission business in Augsburg fustians, adding a trade in other textile products, especially in fine damasks, brocades, and other silk stuffs of Italian origin. In addition he imported from Italy fruits, saffron, spices, precious and semiprecious stones, and other products of the Italian peninsula, the Levant, far India, and eastern Asia.

It was of the greatest significance that the older brothers also entered into financial relations with the papacy and the Emperor. While Jacob, born in 1459, was still a student of theology, Ulrich and George were in 1475 transferring to Rome the receipts of the Papal See, collected by the papal representatives in Scandinavia. The transfer by the Fuggers of papal privileges to interested parties in Germany, through the Roman representatives of the Fugger firm, had begun even earlier, at least by 1472.

Ulrich also prepared the path for Jacob in the matter of financial transactions with the temporal princes, especially the Habsburgs. Inevitably, in view of the financial needs of the Habsburgs, the purveying of textiles, into which we saw Ulrich entering in 1473 with Emperor Frederick III, developed into the advancing of credit. From this to direct loans was an easy step. To be sure, the loans to the Habsburgs and other princes took on larger dimensions only after Jacob had entered into the leadership of the business alongside Ulrich and George, but the way had been prepared.

Even the development of certain principles of the internal legal organization of the Fugger enterprise was begun under Ulrich. The tendency, for example, to exclude all those not of Fugger blood from the trading company, later developed to the last degree by Jacob, was to some extent begun by Ulrich. Long-standing business and trading relations, in themselves quite satisfactory, were sacrificed to this principle by the older brother. The Fuggers of the Lily had been for years, perhaps for decades, connected with the Nuremberg merchant Hans Kramer in a special trading company. This was dissolved by Ulrich and his brothers in 1486, forcing Hans Kramer out of the enterprise at Nuremberg, so that its growing profits might be retained in the hands of the Fuggers alone. George became the manager of the important Fugger factory at Nuremberg, and the Fugger trading company had achieved that measure of exclusiveness which Jacob considered necessary for his work.

CHAPTER IV

YOUTH AND APPRENTICESHIP; THE RISE TO LEADERSHIP

J ACOB FUGGER II, later known as "the Rich," was born on March 6, 1459, the son of Jacob Fugger I and his wife Barbara, née Bäsinger, in the old Fugger house in Augsburg, located in that section of the city called "vom Ror." The house stood opposite the imposing gild house of the weavers, in the chief trading street of Augsburg. Jacob was the tenth among eleven children, and the youngest of seven brothers.

His father, about whom we unfortunately know very little, was counted among the most prosperous men of the city. Through the use of the tax-books of Augsburg for various years of the fifteenth and sixteenth centuries, the author has been able to work out a hierarchy of the richest people in the old imperial city. The elder Jacob Fugger by the middle of the fifteenth century belonged in the first rank. In 1461, shortly after the birth of his youngest son, the amount of his property was exceeded by that of only about a dozen of his fellow burghers. From then on it increased so rapidly that in 1467 he ranked about seventh in old Augsburg. The second place at that time belonged to Lucas Welser, a member of that merchant family which, next to the Fuggers among Augsburg merchants, is the best known to history. His property was almost double that of Jacob Fugger, a relationship which was within a short time to be reversed.

We see here substantially the same phenomenon as in the nineteenth century. The great German economic leaders arose as a rule not from the poorer classes of the people, but from the more prosperous burghers, well established for several generations.

But property was not the only inheritance which the clever elder Jacob Fugger left to his great son and his other children at his premature decease. He had also achieved a highly respected position through his successful, responsible public activity in an honorary capacity for the weavers' gild and the Augsburg community. For the widow this success resulted in many advantageous connections. In the sons, as they grew up, it produced a feeling of self-consciousness and of responsibility for the family thus early robbed of its natural head.

The Widow Barbara first took over the leadership of the Fugger enterprise, as we noted above, and carried it on successfully. In various places the brothers

Ulrich, George, and Jacob have furnished written evidence of their gratitude to the excellent mother and able woman of affairs. During her long life, Barbara Bäsinger experienced both the joys and sorrows of business. She saw that greatest business disaster, bankruptcy, engulf the once prosperous and outstanding house of her father. That may have doubled the widow's eagerness to continue the rise of her new family, the Fuggers of the Lily.

Of the three brothers, Jacob probably knew best what he owed to his exceptional mother. Since he lost his father when he was but ten years old, his mother was responsible for his entire training. It was she, to be sure, who, having in mind the welfare of the whole family and the interests of the business, called the budding theologian out of his study and into the countingroom. And probably the summons was not particularly welcome to the young prebendary. But later at least, if not at the time, Jacob Fugger II perceived it as a natural and justifiable necessity that in a family which is to rise to a position of historical greatness the individual member must subordinate his destiny to that of the whole family. We shall see that Jacob later voluntarily adopted this altruistic and family point of view which was demanded of him by his mother and his older brothers in the change of his calling. And for that reason he could as a mature man, when he had succeeded to the leadership of the Fugger enterprise, demand unrelentingly from the other members of the family that same high conception of family interest and that same sense of duty toward the enterprise.

The exact year when Jacob Fugger attained the position of leadership can scarcely be fixed. The fact that, through his change of calling, he entered upon mercantile training relatively late in life, according to medieval practices, furnishes at least the possibility that masterhood followed very closely upon his period of apprenticeship, which, in accordance with the South German custom of the time, he spent in Venice.

It would seem that it was due to Jacob Fugger's great and rapidly developed mercantile capacity that, during the course of the 1480's, shortly after his return from the Venetian apprenticeship, he began to play an increasingly prominent rôle in the Fugger enterprise, and to take his stand alongside his two older brothers. His wealth grew at the same rate as theirs. When in 1494 the three brothers transformed the older form of the Fugger concern into the more modern one of the trading partnership, in which the three partners bound themselves to invest all their capital and all the profits which the balance then showed, the contribution of Jacob was not greatly exceeded by that of the older brothers. Ulrich invested 21,656 Rhenish gold gulden, George 17,177, and Jacob 15,552 in the Company, which was to continue for six years. It indicates the strengthening of Jacob's position from year to year that he was able in 1502 to carry through a proposal for a gradual equalization of the capital of the brothers, by the allocation of greater profits to George and himself until such time as the capital investments of the three should be the same. In the authority which the agreement of association of 1494 accorded to the three members there was also no discrimination against the youngest brother. Ulrich, to be sure, as the eldest brother, gave the Company its name—the firm name was Ulrich Fugger and Brothers, of Augsburg—but Ulrich was toward Jacob only *primus inter pares,* the first among his peers. The contract of 1494 expressly specified that each of the three brothers should have full power in all questions of trade, in purchase and sale, in the hiring and discharging of subordinates, etc., just as though he were the head of the business.

Although legally, according to the wording of the agreement, the three members were quite equal, actually Jacob's position during the last years of the fifteenth century gradually developed to one of leadership. Their contract gave each one the right to take the initiative in any business move. In fact, however, it was usually Jacob who, because of his business ability, took the first step in anything new and important that was entered upon. He became the determining factor in the growth of the Fugger enterprise.

For the closing years of the fifteenth century, we have no proof of the growing leadership of the young-est brother other than that he always appears to be. the most active. In the Tyrol, the most important *locale* of the widely branched Fugger enterprise, and the most profitable center of their undertaking, Jacob was the leading figure from the end of the 'eighties. He took an equally leading position later in Hungary, which because of its mineral resources became more and more, from the end of the fifteenth century on-ward, the chief foundation of the Fugger fortune. The reins of the increasing business of money-lending also lay chiefly in the hands of Jacob. In addition to all these tasks, the insatiable worker carried on per-sonally the very profitable though exacting work of supervising the books and accounts of the various Fugger factories. Apparently Jacob actually traveled around to the branch offices himself in order to receive the accounts and to observe the business organiza-tion on the spot, where the whole situation could be taken in.

Indubitable proof that Jacob had become the lead-ing spirit of the Fugger enterprise is vouchsafed us from the early part of the sixteenth century. At the

beginning of the year 1503, the chancellor of Duke
Wilhelm of Henneberg sent a query to a member of
the family of the Fuggers of the Roe as to where
the three members of the firm Ulrich Fugger and
Brothers, of Augsburg, could be reached either by
letter or in person in the matter of a financial transaction. The reply to the chancellor was that Ulrich
was in Augsburg, George at the Nuremberg fair, and
Jacob at the Frankfurt fair. They were soon to meet
again in Augsburg. But if the chancellor or his lord,
Duke Wilhelm of Henneberg, wished to do any business with the Fuggers, it would be best to go to Jacob,
the youngest of the brothers, as he was the real head.
The two older brothers never undertook anything of
business importance without him.

Thus it was plain even to outsiders by this time
that Jacob was the leading spirit of the enterprise.
From 1500 onward, anything of importance that hap-
pened in the Fugger Company, whether it had to do
with an extension of the enterprise, or its inward
strengthening by means of family policy, may be
considered as the work of Jacob. In the latter field,
Jacob's greatest achievement was the reorganization
of the Company on an even more aristocratic basis,
protecting it against relatives who were not sufficiently interested in the business, but who had a
selfish interest in inheritance. Connected with this

was the farsighted preparation for his later despotic control of the business as against the sons of his brothers. In this respect, Jacob's labor of decades was a masterly accomplishment of the first rank. The whole family policy was subordinated to the provision for the longest possible maintenance of the enterprise. In comparison with this demand, all other desires and wishes had to be submerged. Jacob looked upon himself only as the first servant of the enterprise. Out of this conception was developed a business organization the like of which is not to be found in economic history.

CHAPTER V

THE BUILDING UP OF THE FUGGER TRADING COMPANY BY JACOB FUGGER. HIS FAMILY POLICY IN THE INTEREST OF THE ENTER-PRISE

IN 1510, after the death of his sole remaining brother, Ulrich, the Fugger enterprise came under the absolute domination of Jacob, possibly without any opposition on the part of his nephews, certainly without any effective opposition. This was the result in part of Jacob's dominating personality; but it was due more to the farseeing policy which he had for decades been consciously pursuing within the family in regard to the business. When his father died in 1469, Jacob, who was then but ten years old, naturally had no influence on the legal form in which the paternal business was carried on in common by the widow and children. Apparently the enterprise took the coparcenary form (*Ganerbenschaft*) common in such cases in South Germany at that time. This meant that those heirs who were both fit for and inclined toward the carrying on of the business did so for the good of all—the widow, the sons, and daughters of the deceased head of the family.

Just when this coparceny ceased, it is impossible to ascertain. It must have been sometime before 1494. The three brothers entered—in just what year is uncertain—into a union which in its legal form was distinct from the preceding coparceny, but in which (in contrast to the private trading partnership—*offene Handelsgesellschaft*—formed in 1494) the property belonging to the mother remained undivided, a part of the capital for profit or loss. Apparently it was Jacob Fugger who in 1494 changed this somewhat · vague transition form into the new one, according to which only the three brothers had capital in the enterprise. This assumption is supported by Jacob's later business policy, which is foreshadowed here. As early as the agreement of 1494, but much more clearly in the contract of 1502, that document so important for the future development of the family, can be seen the beginnings of the provision of this farseeing, cautious man against that tendency toward decline and disintegration which threatens every wealthy mercantile family in its later generations. Jacob's efforts were directed particularly toward insuring the continuance of the Fugger enterprise, sound and successful, as long as possible, in the face of death and the division of the property, the abstention of individual family members from business, and their desire to break up the fortune.

This greatest of the Fuggers early learned to place the family enterprise and its future above everything else, and he continued to follow this policy. For three decades he coped with the great and really insoluble problem of how the proud Fugger structure could be maintained intact, or at least be preserved from all too rapid disintegration. Not for him the indifference of the upstart, who works for the present, without too much concern over the future of the business. The rise of the family had gone too far for that, and Jacob had too keen a sense of having grown up in one of the foremost merchant families of Augsburg, too much of a sense of responsibility toward future generations. He was concerned as much with the permanence of the Fugger enterprise as with its greatness.

He lacked also the selfish love of many fathers who have grown rich, and who, leaving out of account the grandchildren and great-grandchildren, think only of leaving the hard-earned riches as a supposed blessing to their children to enjoy in unearned luxury. For Jacob Fugger had no children, a factor of the greatest importance in the development, not only of his own personality, but of the Fugger enterprise as well. Even of nepotism, that unreasoning love of the nephews, which was a frequent mental weakness of highly-placed childless men in his time, Jacob Fugger had no trace.

His family policy with regard to the business was clearly suggested as early as the partnership agreement of 1494, which was expressly concluded in order to "render the business stable." This aim, of securing the future of the enterprise, would be endangered, as the brothers saw then, if, in case of the death of one of the three, his heirs were given the possibility of creating difficulties for the remaining two associates, and of hindering them in their business arrangements. So it was specified that in case of the death of one or even two of the associates, their heirs should leave the capital in the business for three years, and even after that were to be satisfied with gradual repayment. The heirs, to be sure, during the specified three-year period, were to share in profit and loss, but were to refrain from taking any part in the control of the business. They were even to withhold any comment upon the balance, which the surviving associate or associates were to determine.

This 1494 agreement of the three brothers, which was to last only six years, seems to have been extended for some time beyond 1500, by oral agreement. The next change in the legal organization of the Company took place at the end of 1502. From·

that time forth, Jacob was the accepted leader. The most outstanding tendency expressed in these significant contracts of December 23 and 24, 1502, was along the line of ensuring, so far as possible, the permanence of the Fugger greatness. Jacob thought this could best be achieved by strengthening the leadership of the enterprise. In the future, it was to be governed aristocratically, that is, by a few highly privileged masculine members of the family. It was naturally a matter of some importance which one among the men in any generation should have this control. Jacob took special measures to ensure the permanent interest of the ablest in the business. Very astutely this unrivaled strategist made use of the interests which the Fugger Company had recently acquired in Hungary, and other mining privileges and smelting works—more detailed reference will be made to them in the later chapter on Jacob Fugger in Hungary—in order to carry out his farseeing plans. "In order that our name and family and our male heirs and successors shall the more steadfastly remain in trade;" in order further that the Fugger enterprise "shall not be broken up and destroyed by over-diffusion and we or our heirs thereby suffer," the three brothers, Ulrich, George, and Jacob, at the end of 1502 took the following decisive steps. The interests in Hungarian and other mines and smelting plants, already acquired or still to be acquired, were to be reserved for the male heirs of the three brothers; that is, should be withheld from the general inheritance. Only if there were no legitimate male heir of the three brothers living could the female members of the family enter into the inheritance. Even the male heirs of the Fuggers, if in the ecclesiastical orders, were excluded from this part of the inheritance.

The male descendants did not enter into the inheritance of this special and important part of the property without reciprocal duties and obligations. They might in no way, either by sale or by mortgage or the like, alienate any part of this "Preferred Share" (*Voraus*). Further, all those who participated in it were bound to leave their whole business capital, together with the profits earned, in the Fugger enterprise. If one or the other wished to withdraw—which was quite contrary to the wishes and the plans of the three brothers—he must sacrifice his share in the "preferred holding."

In addition to the interest in Hungarian mining and smelting, other items of value were applied to strengthening the capital of the Fugger enterprise and to fasten the successive generations to the business. Certain houses and pieces of property in Augsburg and its environs inherited by the three brothers

in common, or purchased with common funds, were
to pass on only to their male successors who were
active in the business. Similarly with silver vessels,
tapestries, and other costly house furnishings, already
bought or to be bought, which were applied to the
decoration of the above-mentioned houses. These items
of property and objects of value were also to be withheld from sale, at most exchangeable for other objects
of like value. Jacob Fugger was here developing, from
the same motives and aims as actuate family trust
commissions, family policies of lasting value. Later
we shall see him move much further along this
line.

These arrangements do not by any means comprise
the whole of the great contract brought to conclusion at Christmas time, 1502. It was also attempted,
by a careful regulation of the future leadership of
the Fugger enterprise, to ensure the continuance of
trade "in good and steadfast fashion." If one of the
three brothers died, the other two, without opposition
from his heirs, were to govern the prosecution of the
business absolutely. The two "directors" of the business, however, were to choose as a substitute from
among their sons and nephews the one most fitted
for trade to educate him in the business, so that in
case of the death of the second brother, the remain-

ing one would have help in carrying on the business. If the last of the three brothers died, two "directors" should be chosen from among the next generation of the family, and a third should be educated in business as a substitute. For all the future, the aristocratic. principle of absolute domination by two "directors" was established, against every opposition from the other members of the family.

It was the duty of the two "directors" to place. all available male members of the family in trade. If one of the "directors" were disobedient, the other might force the refractory member out of the circle of the fully privileged and reduce his share of the profit by 33⅓ per cent. As an extra reward, the "directors" were to draw 2 per cent in advance from the profits. Their presumptive successor, the substitute, was to receive 1 per cent.

Only two safety valves were provided in the contract of 1502 against possible injurious effects of the absolutism of the two "directors." In case one of them misused his extraordinary power to the obvious injury of the business, his co-director, together with the substitute, should apply to the other members of the family, and by a majority decision a change could be introduced. In the second place, it was forbidden to the "directors" to alienate anything from the "Preferred Share." This might occur only with the knowledge and consent of the majority of the privileged members. The participation of this majority was also necessary for new purchases, in case large sums were involved.

CHAPTER VI

THE RISE OF JACOB TO COMPLETE DOMINA-
TION IN THE FUGGER ENTERPRISE. HIS CARE
FOR THE FUTURE

THE chief provision with regard to the future
leadership of the Fugger enterprise, as determined in the contract of 1502, was that after the death
of the three brothers, Ulrich, George, and Jacob, the
Company should be controlled by two of their male
successors as "directors." Complete domination by one
man should rest in the hands of only the last one of
themselves to survive. It was natural to expect that
this would be Jacob, by far the youngest of the three.
As a matter of fact, death, which in the case of
George took no account of the relative ages of the
brothers, vouchsafed to Jacob the full span of life.
He survived George, who died in 1506, by almost
twenty years; and Ulrich, who passed away in 1510,
by fifteen years.

During these fifteen years, the actual leadership of
Jacob in the Company was succeeded by the actual
and legal control by this one great merchant alone,

who, thus realizing the full consequences of the contract of 1502, became, as the last survivor, the absolute monarch of the enterprise. What led Jacob Fugger to this line of conduct? Was absolutism natural to his dominating nature, or was it his opinion that only thus could he attain the high aims of his business imperialism? Was he perhaps unable to decide which of his nephews was fitted for co-direction? Did he wish to try them all out first, before he elevated any of them to co-directorship? Or did he wish to train all his nephews in complete subordination to the business and its leadership, so that when they, after their uncle's death, succeeded to control, they would be prepared to carry through the same policy with respect to those members of the family not admitted to leadership? Was it perhaps a practical apprenticeship in the value and importance of mercantile absolutism which Jacob wished to assure to the future generations of his family?

We shall probably never know which one or ones of these motives actuated the great merchant. In any case, during the last and most interesting period of his life (1510 to 1525), he pursued this policy of unlimited domination of the enterprise, dauntlessly, even though perhaps sometimes daunted by the timid attempts at opposition on the part of his nephews. None of these was successful in the attempt to place himself beside his uncle as co-director. Indeed, they did not even become associates in the places of their deceased fathers. Although the male heirs were naturally required to leave their inherited capital for profit or loss in the business—the female heirs were paid off on the basis of an approximate balance which Jacob struck immediately after the death of Ulrich—they had no share in its direction.

With the greatest strictness, excluding all family feeling, Jacob in 1510, the year of Ulrich's death, secured a solemn confirmation in legal instruments of the subordination of his nephews to his autocratic rule, strengthening this by an oath upon the Bible. Seldom has a ruler humbled a crown prince so deeply as this ruler of wealth did his nephews and successors. What a range of synonyms for absolute authority he collected in these instruments to testify to his unlimited power in the business! What pleonasm we find there, which all goes to make clear the position that his nephews were to enjoy as toward him. And this position was one less privileged than that often enjoyed in other enterprises by clerks not even bound to their chief by ties of blood.

At last Jacob thought best to give a new legal expression to his power and his designs for the future leadership of the Fugger enterprise. Accordingly, on December 30, 1512, Jacob declared terminated the agreement concluded between himself and his brothers Ulrich and George in 1502. According to the same instrument, "he took over the business for himself," and at their request, took into the business for six years his nephews, Ulrich and Hieronymus, the sons of Ulrich, Sr., and Raimund and Anton, George's sons. The new firm name was "Jacob Fugger and Nephews," in Italian, "Jacobo Fugger e nepoti." The nephews, during the course of the contract, were to leave the whole of the capital employed by their fathers in trade, together with the profits, in the Company. On his own volition, Jacob might, on the termination of this contract in 1518, extend it for six years longer. He could also alter it at will. Whenever he wished, he could dissolve the Fugger Company and pay off the nephews on the basis of a balance which he alone had the right to draw up. Even the heirs of the nephews had no right to demand a reckoning of any kind from Jacob.[1]

According to this contract, the nephews appear to have many obligations, but very few rights, as against the all-powerful leader of the business, and to be bound to unconditional obedience. They have no right of procuration. For all business injuries caused, they are liable. For all Jacob's dealings they are jointly responsible with him. At any time, he is

[1] See Articles of Association, pp. 189 ff.

free to dismiss them or pay them out. He is in every respect the master. Again and again in this contract of December 30, 1512, and in its supplements, which relate to the Hungarian mining business and to the landed property, he refers to "my trade." "I" is the dominant word in these contracts.

Jacob even went so far as to arrange for his nephews and their fate in the Fugger trading company after his death. If he dies during the period of the contract, his two oldest nephews, Ulrich, Jr., and Raimund, are to take his place as directors, with similar absolute power. In such a case, Jacob's heirs may not question the balance which is to be drawn up by the two directors within one and one-half years after his death. The money is to be paid out on the installment plan within three years to his heirs. If in these last provisions, Jacob placed the interests of the concern above those of his heirs, even of his wife, this predominant interest stands out even more clearly in the arrangements which he made at the same time concerning the share of the Fugger firm in mining and smelting in Hungary, and in the landed property. During the time before the death of Ulrich, the brothers had greatly increased the landed holdings of the Fuggers. The family had acquired houses, gardens, and other holdings in and around Augsburg, but they had entered the ranks of the large landed proprietors of Swabia especially through the acquisition of imperial holdings. This immense, newly acquired landed property was also reserved to the male descendants—with indemnification of the females—according to the old arrangements of 1502. If Jacob wished to increase this landed property, he was free to do so. During his lifetime, he had the administration of this whole common possession of the males in the family of the Fuggers of the Lily. He might sell any part of it; but even he bound himself to the observation of the fundamental principle of inalienability of this part of the Fugger business property in so far as he agreed to make full substitution in case of sale.

As we saw, there were, in the agreements of December 23 and 24, 1502, provisions for the way in which the next generation of the family should conduct the business. Now in 1512, Jacob provided that Ulrich and Raimund might be taken on by him, one—not yet specified—as "director," the other as apprentice. The All-Powerful retained the right, however, to recall this choice and to choose other nephews for these posts. The participation of the nephews, further, was to place no limits of any kind on the power of the uncle. During his lifetime, "the whole and complete power rested in him alone."

The family policy of Jacob Fugger finds its conclusion in his two wills. The first of them is dated

1521; the latter, just a few days before his death, December 22, 1525. In these last dispositions of the aging man, as heretofore, the leading place is occupied by his wish that the business be carried on as long into the future as possible by "the Fugger family and name." He makes larger or smaller bequests to his wife and to his nearer female and more distant male relatives; but his chief heirs are his four nephews, the heirs of the Fugger business. To them falls all the business property and the personal property, so far as it is not deeded away in bequests. To them belongs the oft-mentioned "Preferred Share" in the Hungarian mining business and in the landed property.

So great is his concern for the welfare of the business that he hesitates over the size of his bequests and considers the danger of too great a capital-withdrawal, especially in the case of unfavorable business conditions. Certain legacies are to be cut down, or even entirely abandoned, in case the Hungarian enterprise, already endangered by the Turks and by political conditions, sustains heavy losses; or in case the loans to the Emperor bring great losses to the trading company. The decision in this matter is to be made by the two oldest nephews, Ulrich and Raimund, who are specified as the directors of the business, with special rights as against their younger brothers.

This important problem of succession in the direction of the enterprise engaged Jacob's attention until the end of his life. The question was complicated first by the death of Ulrich shortly before that of his great. uncle. It was made still more difficult by the fact that Ulrich's brother Hieronymus did not remain in the business. Hence Jacob arranged that Ulrich's quarter in the "Preferred Share" and in the inheritance from his uncle should not go to his brother Hieronymus, but that each of the three nephews should receive one third of the inheritance. Hieronymus was entirely excluded from direction of the business. In the Hungarian trade, Raimund and Anton were to represent the Fugger trading company with equal rights, but in the rest of the business Anton was to decide and govern alone as absolute director, like his uncle before him. From his control was removed only the oft-mentioned common property, which Jacob had increased, not only by land, but also by valuable jewels. For their directive activities, Raimund and Anton were to receive 12½ per cent of the annual profit (from 1511 onward) of the business. Hieronymus was also excluded from the 5 per cent which was to fall to the directors as an extra return from the profits of the "Hungarian trade." One can clearly see in these arrangements of Jacob his efforts to deflect the bulk of the property to those lines where the future of the family obviously lay, for Hieronymus was childless.

That part of Jacob Fugger's policy which we have already traced may be considered the purely family side of his policy. There was on the other side his conduct toward relatives by marriage and toward old, deserving business associates, so-called factors. This policy comprised, putting it simply, relentless elimination of all these non-Fugger elements, which tended naturally to penetrate the leadership of the enterprise.

In carrying out this policy, Jacob Fugger stood in contrast to almost all the trading companies of his time. It was characteristic of most of the great South German trading companies of the fifteenth and sixteenth centuries either that from the first, members of different families were associated, or that they gradually lost the character of purely family undertakings by taking in as associates relatives by marriage and old factors. Jacob Fugger consciously avoided this policy, which led to continuous strife in the leadership of the company. Foreign blood was excluded from the Fugger enterprise as a matter of principle. In this respect also, the organization created by Jacob in the Fugger Company was something individual, and was recognized by clever mercantile contemporaries as worthy of imitation; this organization, however, was nowhere else achieved in its completeness.

CHAPTER VII

THE BUSINESS SUCCESS OF THE FUGGER ENTER-
PRISE UNDER JACOB'S LEADERSHIP. PAR-
TIAL INVESTMENT OF THE EARNINGS IN
LANDED PROPERTY

THE financial results of Jacob Fugger's work stand
out with impressive clarity from the inventory
and balance arranged for by Anton Fugger shortly
after the death of his great uncle. Completed in the
year 1527, this inventory has fortunately been preserved down to the present. The great merchant was
eminently successful, first as co-worker and then as
director, in making the Fugger business the most
important and wealthiest trading house of its time.
Between 1494 and 1525 the capital of the Company
was greatly increased by fortunate profits in trade
and industry. In 1494 the three brothers invested in
their open trading company the following capital:

Ulrich,	21,656	Rhenish gold gulden
George,	17,177	" " "
Jacob,	15,552	" " "
Total,	54,385	" " "

Seventeen years later, when Jacob made a reckoning
of profits in order to settle with the female heirs of
his deceased brother, the reckoning was not made on
the basis of an inventory and an ordinary balance.
Instead, Jacob estimated the profits for each year at
an average of 15 per cent. It is not likely, astute business man that Jacob was, that this estimate was too
high. He was too much interested in the business,
which would be weakened by an over-withdrawal of
capital, and too little interested in the female side of
the family, which would have had the chief benefit
from too high a percentage, to make such a mistake.
We have to do, in this estimated 15 per cent yearly
profit, with a minimum rather than a maximum. Of
the landed property and houses, we know without
question that they were appraised only at their purchase price, and that all the improvements, for instance, which Jacob had introduced were not included.

On the basis of his estimate, Jacob Fugger then
(February 14, 1511) reckoned the Fugger business
property at the following figures:

Fixed property, houses,
   house furnishings,
     silver,   70,884 Rhenish gold gulden

Outstanding assets, goods, money, and valuables,	213,207	Rhenish gold gulden		
Total,	284,091	"	"	"
From this must be subtracted for endowments,	15,000	"	"	"
Balance,	269,091	"	"	"

From this, after a provisional payment of 39,800 gold gulden to the female heirs of Ulrich and of 32,500 gold gulden to those of George, there remained in the trade on a new reckoning the following sums:

Jacob's capital,	88,875	Rhenish gold gulden		
Capital of Raimund and Anton,	52,257	"	"	"
Capital of Ulrich and Hieronymus,	55,659	"	"	"
Total,	196,791	"	"	"

This balance formed the starting point when, after the death of Jacob Fugger, it was necessary to reckon the profits of the business between 1511 and 1527. According to the inventory of the latter year, which

was made with the greatest care under the leadership
of Anton Fugger, and which was an inventory, not
an estimate, the capital of the enterprise on December
31, 1527, was:

In fixed property,	127,902	Rhenish gold gulden		
In outstanding assets, goods of all kinds,	1,904,750	"	"	"
Total,	2,032,652	"	"	"
From this must be subtracted for endowments,	11,450	"	"	"
Leaving as the capital of the Company on December 31, 1527,	2,021,202	"	"	"

If one subtracts from this 196,791 Rhenish gold
gulden, the capital of the undertaking on February
14, 1511, there remains as profit for the seventeen
years 1511–1527 the impressive sum of 1,824,411 gold
gulden. This tenfold increase of the invested capital
means an average profit of 50 per cent a year. But
though Jacob Fugger secured these unusually large
profits, the safe and secure investment of all surplus
liquid capital was always his special care. Jacob invested that part of the business capital which could

be dispensed with in the conduct of the greatly expanded business itself partly in jewels and silver, but mainly in landed property. In 1511, the investments of the Fugger enterprise in landed property, houses, and valuables were appraised at a very low estimate, at 70,884 Rhenish gold gulden. In 1527, the corresponding figure had already reached 127,902 gold gulden.

The Fugger estates which Jacob had acquired were partly urban, but mainly rural, and consisted predominantly of large estates. In 1507, he bought from the Emperor Maximilian the Duchy of Kirchberg in Swabia, together with the Swabian domains of Wullenstetten and Pfaffenhofen, and Weissenhorn with Mauerstetten and Buch, paying 50,000 Rhenish gold gulden. In 1509 he added the Hofmark Schmiechen with its castle, also from the imperial holdings. The purchase price was 3,200 gold gulden. In 1514 followed the acquisition of the domain Biberbach on the Schmutter, not far from Augsburg. This purchase, under imperial mediation, was from the possessions of the Marshalls of Pappenheim, for a price of 32,000 gulden.

All together, the large estates which Jacob acquired in Swabia cost about 92,000 Rhenish gold gulden. The income from them could not have been much over 3,000 gulden; accordingly, the return on the invested

The Fugger Palace in Augsburg

capital must be reckoned at about 3 per cent. This was, of course, not a paying investment in the strict sense of the word. But Jacob was not thinking here of profits in the narrow sense. There is no doubt that Jacob made this investment as a part of his policy, his opinion concerning the importance and the necessity of large landed estates for a bourgeois merchant family differing sharply from those of other descendants of merchants who had grown wealthy. It was not at all Jacob's idea to use these landed estates as the means of satisfying small social ambitions. It was true then, as it is even today, that large holdings of land gave a higher social position than the possession of wealth alone; and it was further true that the purchase of great landed domains made possible an advance into the ranks of the landed nobility, with an opportunity to forget the bourgeois origin. These considerations often led the wealthy bourgeois families in all countries in the Middle Ages and the early modern period to invest in landed estates the capital which they had amassed in trade. A study of the changes in the ownership of the large Swabian domains between the end of the fourteenth and the seventeenth or even the eighteenth centuries would show how the rising Augsburg, Ulm, and Memming merchant families acquired large and small domains, castles, and holdings of the nobility in Swabia. Usually they held them for a time, and then exchanged them for others or, much more frequently, were forced to sell them again. For by no means did all of these bourgeois families which sprang up succeed in establishing themselves and entrenching themselves permanently in the feudal régime. It was easy, during a rapid rise, to acquire large estates, but very difficult to maintain them permanently. The history of many merchant families seems to indicate that the second or third generation forsook urban life. Indeed, oftentimes the son of the fortunate upstart established himself in a mode of life which corresponded to knightly customs and ideas. But often the appearances are deceiving. The rapid rise was frequently followed by an equally rapid decay. As the result of the over-extension of their mercantile enterprises, the insolvency of their princely debtors, or some other such cause, the estates acquired during prosperity often had to be liquidated, in order to satisfy the creditors and to secure fresh business capital. In case this transformation of fixed into liquid capital did not occur with sufficient rapidity, bankruptcy was not infrequently the result of this investment in non-liquid form of funds which should have been kept readily available. The estate passed into the hands of temporarily more fortunate merchants.

The acquisition of landed property for this purpose of satisfying social ambition was always foreign to

Jacob Fugger. So also was the idea of purchasing immense domains in Swabia for the furthering of the fantastic plans of some lofty political ambition. Great was the power of the Fugger House, to be sure, which Jacob had established by the acquisition of feudal possessions. So great indeed, that it justifies the thought that this powerful and wealthy merchant had set up as his final aim the re-establishment of the Duchy of Swabia for the House of Fugger. And a less matter-of-fact temperament than that of Jacob Fugger might well have considered such a plan practicable, especially in the sixteenth century, in a period when the emperor's need of money was extreme and the power of the greatest banker of his time was correspondingly large. What the Medici later achieved—the rise from the Florentine merchant class to be Grand Dukes of Tuscany—need not have appeared impossible to the strong will of a Jacob Fugger.

But such political ambition for himself and his house lay far from Jacob's modest mind. He was too much the merchant, body and soul, and according to his wish, his successors in the family should remain merchants. The granting of nobility (in 1511), and the elevation to the rank of Count was to Jacob Fugger only the means to make possible the assertion of all the rights of the newly-acquired domains in Swabia. The motive which guided Jacob when he acquired for the Fugger family these immense landed estates was really a dual one. In the first place, he wished, by the investment in land of a greater or lesser portion of the Fugger capital, to avoid some of the risks of changes in mercantile fortune; and especially to escape the always extended hand of the royal financial agents. What was thus invested could not disappear in the bottomless pit of the Habsburg financial policy!

In the second place, Jacob Fugger undoubtedly acquired and held large estates for the sake of increasing the fame of his trading house. He well knew that nothing could strengthen his credit more than the obvious and striking impression of wealth conveyed by large holdings of land. Was it perhaps the experience of the Italians which Jacob Fugger, along with many other German merchants of the fifteenth and sixteenth centuries, here utilized? It is well known that the Florentine and other bankers of medieval Italy deliberately tried to increase their credit and their mercantile renown at home and abroad by the acquisition of estates as the most concrete expression of their property and wealth and as producing the most visible impression. We know how strongly Machiavelli leaned to the view that only that merchant who acquired land could ensure his permanent prosperity.

Was Jacob Fugger here also the apprentice of the

Italians? Or does the tradition of the quiet, crafty merchant which Jacob Fugger was here following reach much further back into antiquity, to the mercantile wisdom of the Orient, as it was represented and developed primarily by Jewry? The sayings of old Hebraic scribes and the mercantile wisdom tested by the changing fortunes of Jewish traders through the ages furnish the counsel to divide one's property into three parts, and to invest one in land, the second in jewels and precious metals, and to keep only the third part, though it may be the largest, in ready money always available for trading purposes.

CHAPTER VIII

THE INTERNATIONAL MERCHANT

IN THE economic history of Germany in the six-teenth century, which has yet to be written, one of the most fascinating chapters will concern itself with the story of the rapidity with which the South German merchants learned the economic value of the Portuguese and Spanish discoveries and conquests. Italy, with its chief commercial center, Venice, in spite of the altered conditions in the world spice trade, still continued during the sixteenth century to in-crease in absolute significance as far as the South German merchants were concerned. But in addition, Spain and Portugal now became important scenes of· their activity. From the time that the Portuguese fleets began to bring the Indian spices to Europe over the direct sea route from Africa, Lisbon became the· leading spice market of the Occident. The Portuguese government, which controlled the Indian trade chiefly as a state monopoly, reaped extraordinary profits. Alongside, and soon superseding, Lisbon as the chief center for the spice trade appeared the more favorably situated Antwerp. This development began when the Portuguese established a royal factory there, which handled the spice contracts with the merchants of various nationalities who sought out the city on the Scheldt. These spice treaties, or pepper contracts, as they were called in the sixteenth century, provided that the contractors should supply the king in advance over a specified period with the purchase price of a certain quantity of spices. Upon the arrival of the Indian fleet, the royal debt would then be repaid in the agreed product. The widely fluctuating market price of the goods, the long lapse of time between the setting of the purchase price and the determination of the selling price, the frequent monetary losses of the Portuguese king, along with other factors, made these spice contracts rather speculative undertakings. Consequently Jacob Fugger did not find in them, as many another South German merchant did, a favorite and frequently sought out field for his entrepreneurship and his capital. Instead, he declined spice speculations on a large scale, although he more than once had the opportunity for them. The Fuggers had ranked subordinate to other South German firms in the spice trade in Venice; the same was now true in Lisbon and Antwerp. The Welsers, for instance, played a rôle in Portugal quite different from that of the Fuggers during the lifetime of Jacob the Rich. To be sure, this greatest of Augsburg merchants was not entirely unknown in the Antwerp factory of the king of Portugal, in the Indian House at Lisbon, or in the spice markets of the two cities. This was inevitable, if for no other reason than that so great a dealer in silver and copper as Jacob Fugger was in a position to supply first-hand the commodities of exchange most desired in India.

Jacob Fugger also took a limited part in the direct exploitation of the Portuguese conquests in India. When in 1505 a consortium of Augsburg firms received permission from the king of Portugal to equip royal ships for the trip to India at their own risk, in return for a share in the profits of the Crown, the firm which participated the most heavily was not the Fuggers, but the Welsers. The profit secured by this consortium was extraordinarily great. Although neither the Fuggers nor the other South German merchants participated further to any considerable extent in the Portuguese trips to India, this was not due to their lack of interest, but rather to the absolute monopolization of the Indian trade in the hands of the Portuguese state.

In Spain, also, we first find Jacob Fugger comparatively late and at a time when other South German firms, the Welsers especially, had long been on a solid footing there. The credit which was extended by Jacob for the election of Charles v as Emperor was secured, at least partly, by Spanish Crown revenues. And it was the collection of this debt which first led the Augsburg merchant deeply into Spanish financial administration. Jacob was thus more or less forced into those business relations in which later, long after his death, his House was to suffer such heavy losses.

What Jacob Fugger attempted in Portugal at the beginning of the sixteenth century with rather limited means—to secure a direct share in the colonial administration of the country—he undertook again in the 1520's with Spain. In September, 1520, Fernão de Magalhães returned home after three years from his first trip around the world. During the course of the voyage, he had taken possession for Spain of the Moluccas, those fabulous Spice Islands, from which heretofore even the Portuguese had secured the precious products only indirectly. Charles v then developed a scheme to enter upon a sharp competition with the Portuguese drug trade, with the help of this new possession. The German merchants also laid great hopes on this new territory of their Emperor. Jacob Fugger became their spokesman and requested from Charles v, on behalf of himself and the German merchants, the privilege of participation in the Molucca voyage by equipping ships. The permission was actually given. The Fuggers invested rather large sums-in the expedition led by Garcia de Loaisa; and Jacob Fugger also evidently invested capital in the voyage which Sebastian Cabot shortly afterward undertook on behalf of Spain. But it was only after the death of Fugger, in January, 1526, that Garcia de Loaisa left the Spanish coast, to be followed still later by Cabot. So Jacob Fugger was spared the knowledge of the complete failure of both expeditions, a failure to which the Fugger inventory of 1527 bears testimony to the extent of 4,600 irrecoverable Spanish ducats.

Jacob Fugger achieved more success in Spain with the mortgage of the so-called Maestrazgos, that is, the pledging of the incomes of the Spanish Crown from the three religious orders of Santiago, Calatrava, and Alcántara. The mortgage was made over to Jacob Fugger by Charles v to cover the loans made at the time of the imperial election. The Fuggers controlled the Maestrazgos for almost a century, against renewed loans. This fact alone indicates that it was not an unprofitable pledge which Jacob brought to his House at the beginning of the year 1525. These new Spanish connections were of importance for the position of the Fugger enterprise with relation to European industrial development, since to the Maestrazgos belonged—in addition to extensive agricultural properties—the quicksilver mines of Almada. From this field of mining enterprise, which the Fuggers improved in important respects, they later won rich profits over a long period.

It may thus be seen that until the year of Jacob Fugger's death, his enterprise was of only moderate importance in Spain and Portugal. In France, it figured even less prominently. In Lyons, the French center for the activity of South German merchant houses, the Fuggers had at that time no counter at all. Jacob Fugger had no share in the finance which developed there, making that center, next to Antwerp, the greatest bourse of the sixteenth century. While other Augsburg firms, and especially Nuremberg firms, were developing an active exchange and credit business in Lyons, and were also placing their resources in growing measure at the command of the French Crown, Jacob Fugger held back. This attitude is to be explained by the opposition between the Houses of Habsburg and of Valois, and from the fact that Jacob Fugger, in outward policy and from inward inclination, was completely aligned with the Habsburgs.

The chief weight of the Fugger enterprise thus lay in the Holy Roman Empire, and in the lands of the European East. Italy was also important, Venice and Rome constituting the two most important points of Fugger activity. Finally, Antwerp, which from the beginning of the sixteenth century developed rapidly to a world trading center, became an important nucleus for Jacob Fugger's trade, and soon for his finance as well. The Fugger House contributed to the great stream of goods flowing out of Antwerp especially the rich ores which were transported from the German, Austrian, and Hungarian mines via the Weichsel, the Oder, or the Elbe, or through the Baltic or the North Sea, or perhaps over the land route through central Europe. In addition, there were the products of South German industry, especially the fustian industry of Swabia. Jacob Fugger's Antwerp factor carried on the manifold and responsible duties of his office in an impressive house, whose splendor Albrecht Dürer admired when he was in the Netherlands. He not only conducted the sale of the commodities just mentioned, but also purchased for his principals those goods of northern and southern Europe, the Levant, and the distant Portuguese and Spanish colonies, for which Antwerp was more and more becoming the market.

The Antwerp factory grew greatly in importance as this city on the Scheldt became the central point for European high finance. The South German financiers appeared in increasing numbers on the Antwerp bourse alongside the Italian, Spanish, and Dutch bankers. For a while, indeed, under the leadership of Jacob Fugger and his successor Anton, the Upper German financiers exceeded all their European com-

petitors in importance. It can fairly be said that Jacob
Fugger was not the least of those who contributed to
the rapid rise of Antwerp as the most important
world market in the sixteenth century.

In many respects, it was under Jacob that Antwerp
began to outrank Venice, that old center of activity of
the Fugger House. That city, to be sure, had never
been of the first importance in international finance,
for the Fuggers any more than for others. For Jacob
Fugger, Venice was only a step toward the exchange
and credit business of Rome. But during the first
decades of the sixteenth century, Antwerp began to
rival Venice in importance for the Fugger goods trade
as well. The Venetian factory of the Fuggers lost in
importance in the pepper trade at least, if not in all
branches of the spice trade. On the other hand, it remained an outstanding center for Fugger's rapidly
increasing export of metals and for the textile im-
ports of his firm. It was chiefly through and from
Venice that Jacob secured the fine silks and velvets
which he as court purveyor supplied in large quantities to the emperor, kings, and princes. The Venetian
factory also handled the Fugger trade in precious
stones and jewels. Not infrequently this involved the
purchase of large and rare diamonds, the value of
which sometimes mounted to 10,000 or even 20,000
Rhenish gold gulden. Very often this traffic with

Venice was carried out in the form of an exchange of fine silks or precious stones for Tyrolese and Hungarian silver and copper.

The Venetian, as well as all other Fugger factories, carried on a very lively business in money-changing. It was chiefly with merchants, who used this means of transferring money from one place to another. But public bodies, cities, princes, and last but not least the Papal See also availed themselves in this way of the net of branches which Jacob Fugger had extended over the whole of Europe. Even private individuals were sometimes served. German miners who had gone to Spain to seek their fortune could send their extra *Groschen* to their relatives in the distant homeland through the new Spanish factory of the Fuggers. Travelers of varying degree in the early sixteenth century often bought letters of credit on one of the Fugger factories, securing cash on them as they needed it from other factories of the House. The international importance which Jacob Fugger had created for his enterprise was expressed thus, as well as in his great financial transactions. At the death of the great Augsburg merchant, there was no other European trading house which had extended its relations as the Fuggers had done, from Scandinavia in the north to Naples in the south, and from England and the Spanish peninsula in the west to Hungary and Poland in the east.

CHAPTER IX

JACOB FUGGER AS CAPTAIN OF INDUSTRY IN THE TYROL AND HUNGARY

WHEN Jacob Fugger in the 1490's attained to the leadership of the Fugger enterprise, it already differed in important respects from that of other Augsburg merchants, who like the Fuggers had risen in the fustian trade and had gradually taken on other branches of trade and also the credit business. The old chronicle of the Fugger House states this fact briefly: Jacob Fugger largely abandoned the fustian and spice trade of his forefathers and "devoted himself especially to mining and exchange." This statement is not literally true; even under Jacob's leadership, trade in fustians and other woven goods, in woolen cloth and fine Italian silks and velvets, as well as in spices, remained an important branch of the many-sided Fugger enterprise. It is true, however, that under Jacob's influence the mining interests, and, along with them inevitably, as we saw above, the credit business gradually assumed the leading place in the Fugger undertaking. At the same time, it is necessary to correct the impression which Charles v expressed in a document of the year 1525, that Jacob Fugger had almost entirely given up all other mercantile pursuits, and had for years occupied himself very largely with mining. It was especially Hungary and the Tyrol which in increasing measure attracted the interest of Jacob Fugger long before the close of the fifteenth century. Until the mines of Spanish America were opened to world trade in the middle of the sixteenth century, these were the two largest silver- and copper-producing areas of the world. It was here that Jacob's enterprise achieved the most brilliant results, here that he developed, further than the majority of the merchants of his day, the rôle of one of the early European captains of industry. This development had taken place in the early years by means of the mines, smelting works, and rolling mills of the Fugger-Thurzo trading company; it was later completed in the Tyrol.

We have seen above how the nearness of the Tyrol, where mining developed rapidly from the second half of the fifteenth century, added to the material prosperity of Augsburg in the age of the Fuggers. With the instinct of the born merchant, the inhabitants of the city on the Lech recognized the possibilities of the situation which offered itself in the mining and the ore trade of the Tyrol. This territory was by no means

new to them. For centuries they had been crossing it
on their trading trips to Italy, especially to Venice.
Now they established themselves more firmly in the
beautiful Habsburg Duchy, so rich in natural resources. To be sure, the active native Tyrolese mining
and smelting entrepreneurs, who did not wish to see
the great profits from the mines of their homeland
pass to foreigners, looked askance at the Swabians.
The Habsburg lords, however, could not dispense with
the financial resources, the entrepreneurship, and the
commercial knowledge of the Augsburg merchants,
if they were to carry on the mining development of
their territory at a rate that corresponded to their
monetary needs. This course of development was determined, at about the beginning of the sixteenth
century, by the House of Habsburg and its desire to
rise to world power, not by the rivalry of the Tyrolese
entrepreneurs or the misgivings of the Innsbruck government.

Thus the Duchy with its natural resources became
a corner stone in the structure of the Augsburg, especially the Fugger, fortunes of this period. Indeed,
the Fugger prosperity from the end of the 1580's was
to a special degree based on the Tyrolese mines. Only
Hungary can in this respect be compared with the
Tyrol in significance for the House of Fugger.

The participation of the Fuggers in the mining of

these two districts was, to be sure, quite different. In Hungary, the Fugger-Thurzo trading company, about which we shall learn more later, acquired by mortgage or purchase a considerable proportion of the most profitable silver and copper mines, and thus as mining proprietors took an outstanding part in the development and the technical improvement of Hungarian mining. This has only recently been recognized, however, by Hungarian historians. In the Tyrol, on the other hand, mining development went on, at least before 1522, without any important direct participation on the part of the Fuggers. It was only after that date that Jacob began to acquire in increasing measure an interest in the Tyrolese mining districts, and to become a real industrialist here, as he already was in Hungary and elsewhere. In the lower Inn Valley, especially in the vicinity of Schwaz and Rattenberg, Jacob Fugger became a very active entrepreneur in the mining of copper and silver. Within a few years, he extended the Fugger mining interests over the whole of North and South Tyrol. In the Lafatsch and Vomper Valleys, in Gossensass and on the Schneeberg (near Ridnaum), at Lienz in the Puster Valley, and at Klausen in the Eisack Valley—in all of these places the Fugger trading company held a larger or smaller number of the mining shares, and had thus an active interest in the mining development. Their smelting works were also to be found at various points in the Tyrol.

As was pointed out above, the Fugger Company had not participated directly in Tyrolese mining before 1522. Before that time, its holdings in the most important mines were of the more purely mercantile type, as some of them continued to be after that date. But in that year, Jacob Fugger acquired important mining holdings in Schwaz, Rattenberg, and Lienz, through the bankruptcy of the Augsburg merchant Martin Baumgartner. The Fugger trading house, in conjunction with the Genoese Antonio de Cavallis (Anton vom Ross), had begun in 1487 to advance money to the rich but ever impecunious Duke Sigmund of the Tyrol, on the security of the Schwaz silver and copper. Thus began for the Fuggers the long-continued series of copper and silver contracts, according to which they advanced a certain sum of money to the Tyrolese duke, receiving in return, until the debt and the interest had been paid in full, the right to take over that share of the minerals which passed to the dukes by virtue of the mining royalties. In this way the Fugger trading company, without itself going into mining, was able to secure at a low price as much silver and copper as it could sell. It goes almost without saying that this entrance of the Fuggers into the marketing of the Tyrolese mining products furnished an important stimulus to the production itself.

The business relationship which Jacob Fugger had thus established with Duke Sigmund of the Tyrol he later continued with his heir, the German King and later Emperor Maximilian I. As a result, the wealthy Hans Baumgartner of Kufstein, formerly the leading financier and purchaser of silver from the Tyrolese Habsburgs, lost this position to the Fuggers. Jacob exploited to the full the favorable political situation which, with Maximilian I, operated against the Bavarian Hans Baumgartner and in favor of the Fuggers, who were burghers of the imperial city. The confidence reposed by the King in the Augsburg business leader increased steadily. In 1491, he secured the preference for his firm in the Tyrolese silver trade. On the basis of reliable information, Max Jansen in his book on the beginnings of the Fuggers[1] estimated their profits in this trade for the years 1487–1494 alone at about 400,000 Rhenish gold gulden. In order to appreciate fully the importance, even for this early period, of this branch of the business, so assiduously cultivated by Jacob, we must add to this figure the profits in the Austrian and Salzburg silver trade (Rauris and Gastein). Jacob Fugger, who was the

[1] Max Jansen, *Die Anfänge der Fugger (bis 1494)*, Leipzig, 1907.

spirit behind this Tyrolese silver trade, seems here to have laid the real foundation for the greatness of his family.

The Fugger trade in Tyrolese copper followed almost the same lines as the silver trade. Long before the Fuggers had begun to participate actively in the mining itself, they were influential in the copper trade. Either alone or in connection with other Augsburg mercantile houses, they traded with the great Tyrolese mining entrepreneurs, and entered into copper contracts with Sigmund and Maximilian I. The metal which they thus acquired they marketed throughout the world, but especially in Venice.

In this trade, too, the profits of the Fuggers were large and on the whole relatively certain. Occasionally, to be sure, there were grave cares connected with it. There were continuous struggles with the dukes and with their hard-headed councilors, who wanted much larger loans than could be covered with the silver and copper receipts. There was a more or less continuous struggle with the Innsbruck government, which saw in Jacob Fugger the most dangerous of those Swabians who were eager to exploit the Tyrol and its resources for their own profit. There were difficulties with the mine workers; and there were market crises and great price fluctuations as a result of oversupply in the copper and silver markets. It can thus be seen that the

profits did not flow into the Fugger coffers from the
Tyrol without any effort on their part. The efforts to
preserve a profitable and, so far as possible, constant
price for copper brought forth against Jacob accusations of monopolistic tendencies, which were given
color by the fact that the Fuggers completely controlled the Hungarian copper region, the second great
producing area of Europe.

The Fuggers were not the first German merchants
to engage in mining, either in Hungary or in the
Tyrol. Rather were they the ones to carry out the
earlier German attempts at economic expansion in
the Magyar districts of eastern Europe. In Hungary,
which became a part of the Holy Roman Empire only
in 1527, it was German miners who in the early
Middle Ages had first begun the systematic exploitation of the ores. And the chief buyers of the products
of the Hungarian mines were the Hanseatic merchants and, in increasing measure from the fifteenth
century onward, South German, especially Nuremberg merchants. The Hanseatic merchants, especially
those from the Prussian city of Thorn, had penetrated
the Hungarian mining district via Crakow, until the
Polish kings, declaring Crakow a staple place, prohibited the Germans from going beyond this city.

A new period of prosperity in Hungarian mining
began in the last quarter of the fifteenth century. Ap-

parently it was a development parallel to that which had taken place on a large scale in the second half of the fifteenth century in the mining of Saxony, the Tyrol, Mansfeld, and related districts, and which in the Carpathians also brought about a revival in the industry, which had become very backward since the end of the fourteenth century. This revival is closely connected with the name of Johann Thurzo, a citizen of Crakow, whose ancestors—perhaps of German origin—had lived in Hungary until Johann moved to Crakow. He seems to have been an expert, such as we often find in the mining districts during the fifteenth and sixteenth centuries, a man who understood how, with the help of a machine driven by mechanical power, a so-called *Wasserkunst* (hydraulic engine), to restore to use mines flooded by water; and who at the same time understood how to make use of the art of separation of metals.

In the older Fugger literature, the opinion used to be expressed that Jacob Fugger during his Venetian apprenticeship had come in contact with Johann Thurzo, who was there to win from the Venetians their secret of the art of separation of metals. According to these sources, the two men at that time agreed upon their later trading company for the exploitation of the Hungarian mines, which was to lead to the association of the two families, so significant for indus-

trial development. Adequate proof of these legends
does not exist. Since scholars had found no evidence of
Thurzo's presence in Germany before this time, or of
that of the Fuggers in Hungary, the Venetian meeting of the two later leaders of eastern European mining industry was assumed. The author has, however,
found proof of the activity of Johann Thurzo as an
engineer in central German mining long before he
and his son associated with the Fuggers, which occurred about the year 1494. In lead mining in the
vicinity of Goslar, Thurzo applied a process by means
of which the copper could be separated from the
copper-bearing lead ore of the Rammelsberg, instead
of smelting the two together as before.

Thus it can be assumed, in view of the international
character of the financing and directing of the mining industry, that the relations of Thurzo and Fugger
could easily have been established elsewhere than in
Venice. The more widespread the fame of Thurzo in
Germany as a mining entrepreneur and engineer, the
more likely that the Fuggers would seek an association
with him, as they knew his work in improving the
technique of mining in the Carpathians. It is naïve to
assume an accidental meeting between Fugger and
Thurzo, especially since quite definite and practical
considerations led Jacob Fugger to seek the association. What a hindrance, for example, the competition

of Thurzo would have been to the Tyrolese copper and silver of the Fuggers in the Italian-Levantine market, if Jacob had had no influence on the growing Hungarian production, which promised much richer yields even than that of the Tyrol.

It was, then, no accident, but constructive talent and an exact knowledge of the conditions of production and marketing which led Jacob Fugger to co-operation with Thurzo. In addition, Jacob Fugger knew the political conditions in Hungary. Never would the patriotic jealousy of the Magyars have permitted the exploitation of the most valuable treasures of the land by the foreigner alone. So the astute German merchant divided the profits which would have been denied to him alone with a family which could be reckoned as native born, one of whose members, Johann, later acquired citizenship in Neusohl and held Hungarian court offices. As was so frequent later, in the nineteenth century, there was united here a native citizen with a foreign capitalist for the economic development of a materially backward land. As so often later, too, there was united in Johann Thurzo and Jacob Fugger the art of the ingenious inventor and the capital resources of the great merchant and financier.

If Jacob Fugger needed Thurzo to make those great profits in Hungarian mining which, together with those of the Tyrol, formed the basis for the European greatness of his trading house, it was no less true that Thurzo needed the Augsburg capitalist. From the contracts which established the terms of their collaboration, from the fact that the Fugger open trading company completely financed the "common Hungarian trade," that is, the Fugger-Thurzo trading company, we can clearly see the dependence of Thurzo on the financial resources of the Fuggers. The Augsburg merchants had to invest enormous sums in the Hungarian enterprise for the equipment of mines and smelting works, for the construction of roads, etc., before a large and continuous profit could be secured. Without the German capital and German entrepreneurship, Hungarian mining, like that of most of the rest of Europe at that time, could not have been developed and carried on with large profits. Of what use to Johann Thurzo that in 1475 the seven Hungarian mining cities of the Carpathian region submitted to him the great problem of freeing the flooded mines from water by the use of his engineering knowledge, in return for a share of the profits? Of what use that the overlord of the land gave his consent and promised the clever technician rich profits? The chief problem in this reconstruction of Hungarian mining was still: Who would invest his capital in the mines and the smelting plants? Who would wish to invest his capital in a land torn by inward strife, against whose borders the Turk stormed with increasing determination? Practically none but a German capitalist would have considered it. But precisely a German might be least attracted by the problem, since the Magyar ruler of the land, Matthias Corvinus, was engaged in a deadly war with the Holy Roman Empire.

The improvement in Hungarian-German relations began only after the Peace of Pressburg, in 1491. This peace further prepared the way for the long-awaited reversion of Hungary to the House of Habsburg. The new Hungarian King, Vladislaw, agreed at Pressburg with King Maximilian I that upon the failure of male descendants, the crown of Stephen should pass to Maximilian and his male heirs. Thus the Habsburgs were at last established in Hungary. Later marriage arrangements further secured the new hope.

On the footsteps of the German King, in Hungary as elsewhere, followed his most outstanding merchant and financier. Within a short time after the signing of the Pressburg Peace, Jacob Fugger undertook the risk of investing large sums in the Hungarian mines. He displayed a farseeing initiative in the economic development of the foreign land. Like Maximilian in his political imperialism, preparing for the political annexation of Hungary, Fugger in his economic im-

perialism established associations with a family which
was rooted in the land—that of the Thurzos. And like
the Habsburgs, too, he sought to fortify his position
in Hungary by marriages. Two members of his immediate family married into the Thurzo family. In
1497 George Thurzo, the son and business associate of
Johann, married Anna Fugger, the eldest daughter of
Jacob's brother Ulrich. In 1513, Raimund Fugger,
the son of Jacob's other brother George, married
Katharina, Johann Thurzo's daughter. With naïve
frankness, the old chronicle of the Fugger family
states that these marriages were "for the furthering
of the Fugger trade."

The legal form by which the private trading partnership of Ulrich Fugger and Brothers, of Augsburg,
joined with the Thurzo Company of Crakow in a
new company, sharply differentiated from both the old
ones, is unusually interesting and a proof of the
marked gift for organization possessed by Jacob
Fugger. In the Fugger business records, this new
branch is referred to as "the common Hungarian
trade," that is, the Hungarian trade in common. This
new enterprise was to carry on the exploitation and
operation of mines, smelting works and rolling mills,
the production of bar silver and copper plate, etc.,
and the sale of these and other goods. The chief cus-
tomers of the Fugger-Thurzo Company were the two

founders, the private trading partnership of Ulrich Fugger and Brothers, and the Thurzo Company. The "common Hungarian trade" sold its mineral and metal products to the Fuggers and to Thurzo, who in turn resold them on their own account; and, on the other hand, it bought from the Fugger enterprise such wares as silks and woolen stuffs and precious stones, either for resale or as presents for the great Hungarian lords, whose favor would be helpful in business.

The business of the Fugger-Thurzo Company had to do overwhelmingly with mining and the metal trade. To it fell the whole mining development of Hungary. It was much more an industrial than a trading enterprise. Jacob was here the controlling spirit among the three brothers, and he appears as a captain of industry much earlier and much more markedly than in the Tyrol. He assumed a leading rôle, in the Tyrol, first in the iron trade, and only indirectly through it influenced the mining industry of the region, even though he later entered directly into mining and the smelting industry. In Hungary, however, the Fugger-Thurzo Company from the first almost completely dominated the mining industry, smelting, and the iron trade of the country. In Upper Hungary (Neusohl, Libethen, etc.), the Company operated partly leased, partly purchased mines. The ore as it was mined was for the most part black copper

(*Schwarzkupfer*), containing more or less silver. That part of it which had the largest silver content—the remainder was sold as copper ore—was smelted in the establishments of the Company, generally in the foundry at Neusohl or at Hochkirch (at St. Georgenthal near Ohrdruf in the Thuringian forest), by blending the black copper ore with lead in great charcoal kilns. The non-fusible lead which resulted, with its silver content, was then allowed to run off from the more rapidly congealing copper, during a gradual cooling of the metal.

The Neusohl smelting and rolling mill was built in 1495 by Johann Thurzo for the Fugger-Thurzo Company. It handled the greater part of the ore produced by the Company in Hungary. A smaller fraction was smelted in the Thuringian plant mentioned above, built for the Company by Jacob Fugger at about the same time. A third smelting plant and rolling mill at Fuggerau, near Villach in Kärnten, which earlier took care of large quantities of the black copper ore (*Schwarzkupfer*) of Upper Hungary, seems in the 1520's to have been supplied only with copper ore from the Tyrol. At this time, the Fuggerau plant served the brass industry mainly. The necessary copper supplies, according to the Fugger inventory of 1527, came from Schwaz in the Tyrol. The requisite zinc was supplied by the Fugger-Thurzo Company from its zinc and lead mines near Villach. A fourth plant, located near Teschen, seems to have been of less importance to the enterprise.

In their mines, smelting plants, and rolling mills, the Fugger-Thurzo Company developed a large-scale enterprise, which gave employment to several hundred workers, in addition to the mercantile activity of the entrepreneurs. Copper was sold in the form of sheets, plates, etc. Silver was a less important article of trade for the firm; the greater part of their production of this metal had to go, according to contract, to the Hungarian mint. The remainder was sold in Nuremberg, Leipzig, Venice, and other centers for the trade in the precious metals.

The starting points of the copper trade of our firm were Neusohl and Hochkirch. The copper trade of the former city was the more important, just as was its production of metal. From Neusohl, the trade was mostly toward western and central Europe. The product went via Oderburg, Breslau, and along the Oder to Stettin, and via Crakow and along the Weichsel to Danzig. At these two termini, the copper was sold by the Fugger-Thurzo Company chiefly to Ulrich Fugger and Brothers, of Augsburg, and their successors. That portion retained by the Fugger-Thurzo Company itself was sold for the most part in Silesia, chiefly in Breslau. That taken over by the Thurzo

Company also remained for the most part in eastern Europe.

The part of the copper taken by the Fugger Company took its course in Hanseatic or Dutch ships through the Sound or via Lübeck and Hamburg to the Netherlands. Here Antwerp was the chief staple place for the copper shipments of the Augsburg firm. But it was not the terminus, for from Antwerp the copper went by ship to Spain, Portugal, France, and even to Italy. It was more common, to be sure, to send the copper of the Fugger-Thurzo firm which was destined for the Italian peninsula over the southern European land route. It would then be transported overseas only from Zengg or Trieste to Venice, and there sold to the Fugger subsidiary. Other centers where the Fugger Company took over the copper from the Fugger-Thurzo Company, in order to resell it on its own account, were the Hochkirch plant and Leipzig. The Fugger Company took over much the largest proportion of the production of the subsidiary company. The Fugger-Thurzo Company itself handled a small fraction; and though we have no figures on the metal trade of the Thurzo Company, it cannot have equaled that of the Fugger firm.

Jacob Fugger was thus the leading spirit in the Fugger-Thurzo enterprise, which earned, during Fugger's lifetime, according to reliable estimates of Max

Jansen, about 1,400,000 Rhenish gold gulden. Of that sum, about 700,000 gulden went to the Fugger firm, and an equal sum to the Thurzo. Jansen further estimates the profits of the Fugger House from the resale of the copper at about 720,000 gulden; and the profit from the goods trade in Hungary at around 80,000 gulden. Jansen estimates the total profit of the Fugger enterprise from the "common Hungarian trade" at 1,500,000 Rhenish gold gulden. As a matter of fact, the profit of the Fuggers must have been considerably more. The Hungarian enterprise was not limited to copper; brass manufacturing and the silver trade flourished as well, especially the latter. In the smelting plants in Hungary, Kärnten, and Thuringia, the Fugger-Thurzo Company produced considerable quantities of silver from the raw copper ore. This was without doubt purchased by the Fugger and the Thurzo firms from their subsidiary. While, to be sure, the profits on this sale fell to the daughter firm, the parent firms must have found substantial profits in the resale of the silver. Unfortunately we do not know the quantity or the price of the silver purchased from the Hungarian company by the Fugger trading house. This prevents any exact estimate of the large sums which must have been drawn from the Hungarian enterprise under the direction of Jacob.

It was of the greatest significance for the price

policy of the Augsburg leader that he almost completely controlled the Hungarian copper and silver
production and the Tyrolese, at least temporarily, to
a very large extent through trade. For a long time
this was the heart of his activity. He naturally sought
to maintain as high a price for copper as the market
permitted. We have already seen that to him, as to
many others of those merchants who led the social and
political life of Augsburg during his time, there was
in such a policy nothing immoral, nothing against
canonical law and its prescription of a just price. He
also made frequent use of his position in Hungary and
the Tyrol for the formation of cartel agreements, the
purpose of which was to raise copper prices or at
least to keep them up. The first occasion was in 1498.
Even at that early date he had ambitions of becoming
soon the only copper contractor for Maximilian 1 in
Schwaz, and thus coming into control in the Tyrol.
At the same time, the Fugger-Thurzo mining enterprise was rising rapidly to unusual heights; and a
world trading monopoly in copper seemed a not impossible achievement for Jacob. Certainly from the end
of the fifteenth century, he was working toward this
aim. In order to secure the leadership in the important Venetian market, he arranged a cartel for the
sale of copper to Venice with Herwart and Gossembrot, two Augsburg merchants with whom in 1496

he had consummated a very large purchase of copper from Schwaz through Maximilian I. The three firms united for the marketing of the 9,600 centners of copper still remaining from this Schwaz purchase. In addition, the selling syndicate also included Hans Baumgartner, the wealthy Kufstein merchant, with 8,000 centners of Schwaz copper, and 8,000 centners of Hungarian copper belonging to the Fugger Company in addition to their share of the 9,600 centners of Schwaz copper. So long as the cartel ran, none of the members was to bring new copper to the Venetian market. The price and conditions of sale of the metal were regulated in detail; the actual sale fell to Hans Keller, the Fugger factor at Venice. Thus as early as 1498, Jacob Fugger appeared to the Venetian metal dealers to be an absolute ruler in the realm of copper. In point of fact, the fall of the cartel soon followed, and he actually became an absolute ruler, at least for a time, as the Schwaz copper came into his exclusive control.

In his wish to create for the Fuggers a world monopoly in copper, through control of the Hungarian and Tyrolese production, Jacob had made the Schwaz copper contract at a higher price than seemed to be justified by the market price at the time. Seen as a part of his whole price policy, however, this was no mistake. Jacob's conduct of the business was from the long-time point of view, and was based on well-considered, mutually interdependent arrangements. He well knew that the balance is struck only at the end of an economic campaign and that it is, therefore, justifiable to pay out at one point if the possibility is thereby created of making the loss doubly good at some other point. As a result of the taking over of the Schwaz copper by the Fugger Company, it was possible for the Hungarian copper of the Fugger-Thurzo Company to seek its most favorable market from the standpoint of transportation. That market lay in western Europe, especially in Antwerp.

For a time, Jacob's plan of creating a world monopoly in copper seemed to succeed. In the first decades of the sixteenth century, the great German merchant was the master, or at least—to make use of the terminology of modern American monopolistic policy—the controller of the two greatest areas of copper production in the world of that day, Hungary and the Tyrol. In Hungary this condition of affairs continued. Jacob's attempts to establish an equally complete domination of the copper mining of the Tyrol went on until his death, without ever achieving any lasting results. Neither the Fugger-Thurzo Company nor the Fugger trading company itself was able to monopolize the Tyrolese copper market completely. Not even the Fugger resources, gradually divided among many interests, sufficed for that purpose and for the immense loans connected with it.

Such a concentration of the Tyrolese copper contracts in the hands of Jacob Fugger was also contrary to the interests of the Tyrolese mining entrepreneurs and of their royal master Maximilian 1. These two powers saw that it was rather to their interests to have several great commercial houses competing for the copper contracts. Such a competition raised the price of the product and made possible larger and more frequent loans from the contractors. The merchants were, to be sure, themselves clever enough to reduce the competition; the strongest candidates often combined in a consortium. In 1515, for instance, the whole copper product of Schwaz, by far the most important in the Tyrol, was granted by Maxmilian 1 for the years 1520–1523 to a consortium composed of the Fugger and the Höchstetter Companies. Naturally this was in return for a large loan. These two companies, as the leading dealers in Tyrolese copper, were thus brought in 1515 to the formation of a cartel, not only participated in heavily, but urged by the Emperor, who as lord of the Tyrol was strongly interested in the maintenance of a high price for copper. In order that the Höchstetters might not be too much dominated in the copper trade by the Fuggers, who absolutely controlled the Hungarian production, the following marketing conditions were agreed upon by the two firms for the marketing of Tyrolese copper: Upper Germany and Italy were to be reserved as a market for Tyrolese copper alone. Hungarian copper, on the other hand, was to be freely imported into the Netherlands.

Jacob Fugger was never entirely successful with his monopoly and his cartel policies, even in the time of their greatest influence and in spite of his great power. He well knew that in following them he rendered himself vulnerable to frequent attacks on the part of public opinion, which was in any case hostile to so new a phenomenon. On this account, Jacob often allowed himself to be defended by imperial and royal declarations and proclamations, to the effect that the contracts for exclusive sale which he concluded with the Tyrolese mining entrepreneurs through the mediation of Maximilian I, especially for the exploitation of Schwaz copper, should not be looked on as monopolistic in the sense prohibited by imperial law. He was playing here the dangerous game engaged in by many of the German merchants of the sixteenth century, a game invented in the first place by the financial advisers of the German kings and emperors of the time in order to fill the empty treasure chests of the Empire at all costs. While in the German Reichstag, since the beginning of the sixteenth century, the lesser political and territorial groups had attacked private monopolies as examples of godless usury, and had provided severe punishments, the German Kings and Emperors Maximilian I, Ferdinand I, and Charles V secretly pledged themselves unconditionally in the monopolistic ore contracts to protect the merchants, in case they were attacked on behalf of the Empire as monopolists. Jacob Fugger experienced only too often how desirable and necessary this insurance was. In 1523 the imperial advocate attempted to make use of the power conferred upon him by the Reichstag and the Emperor. He summoned a number of the Augsburg merchants, Jacob Fugger at their head, before the highest imperial court, to answer for their monopolistic practices. It must have been a sad day for this leading Augsburg family when the messenger of the highest court of the Holy Roman Empire appeared in the famous golden writing room and ceremoniously served the summons on the senior member of the Fugger House, the gray-haired Jacob himself. At the same time, complaints against the monopolistic practices of the merchant prince were publicly announced at the Augsburg city hall. Jacob, as well as the rest of the threatened Augsburg merchants, sought feverishly to avoid the approaching danger. From all sides they drew powerful associates and defenders. In this respect, Jacob Fugger was better placed than the others.

He applied to Duke George of Saxony, with whom he was closely associated in business, and to the Grand Duke Ferdinand, later King and Emperor Ferdinand I. Most especially, he appealed to the Emperor Charles V for help, and not in vain. From Burgos in Castilia, the Emperor directed an energetic letter in the autumn of the year 1523 to the chief advocate, commanding him to drop the suit against the Augsburg merchants at once. At the same time, the Emperor commanded his brother, the Archduke Ferdinand, to suppress the court procedure against the Augsburg merchants.

A year and a half later, Charles V proceeded to regulate the problem of monopoly in principle. Was the Emperor led to this by recognition of his incapacity to preserve the existing condition of affairs? Or did the mercantile class that was concerned force the monarchy to this step? In any case, Jacob Fugger seems to have played a significant rôle. When the general regulation came, his trusted men were working at the Spanish court on the problem of a personal insurance at least of the Fuggers against complaints of monopoly; and there is but little doubt that the Fugger aides also helped to bring about the general regulation. On May 13, 1525, Emperor Charles V issued a mandate from Toledo, voicing the economic doctrine supported by Jacob Fugger, in which he specified that the contracts which concentrated the

wholesale trade in ore in the hands of a few merchants should not be considered as monopolistic in
the sense covered by the Reichstag decrees. Further,
the mining entrepreneurs, or those who had metal
or ore to sell, should have the right to sell their products to one buyer, and to set up in this monopolistic
deal indentures and pacts (*Gedinge und Pacta*), that
is, monopoly contracts with the buyers. The merchants, on the other hand, were naturally free to
enter into such contracts for exclusive purchase. Contrary enactments or provisions of the laws, such as
might have been made or might be made in future by
any person in ignorance of the imperial will, would
be set aside by virtue of imperial sovereignty.

The author has elsewhere discussed the significance
of this highly important imperial decree.[1] Here it is
only necessary to emphasize that the mandate, with
its ethical and economic salvation of the ore trade
monopolies, had in view primarily the Fuggers and
the Höchstetters. It was designed especially to protect
Jacob's attempts at monopoly of Tyrolese copper, and
to save them from antimonopolistic legislation of
both the past and the future.

At the time, Jacob Fugger seems to have had chiefly
two great copper monopoly contracts heavy on his
conscience: the one which he concluded in 1514 for

[1] *Studien zur Geschichte kapitalistischer Organisationsformen,* book ii: *Kirche,
Staat, und Frühkapitalismus.*

his trading house alone with Maximilian I (which ran from Christmas, 1515, to Christmas, 1520), and the one mentioned above, concluded in 1515, in connection with the Höchstetter firm, with the Emperor (to run from Christmas, 1520, until Christmas, 1523). Ten years later, Jacob Fugger considered it worth while to be confirmed by Charles V in the statement that these contracts involved "no unseemly nor criminal enhancement of prices in Germany or elsewhere." Such was the terminology of the mandate issued by the Emperor personally from Toledo on October 26, 1525, for Jacob Fugger and his Company, after he had, on May 13 of the same year, declared monopoly in the field of the ore trade generally to be entirely legal and ethical.[1]

Proof of the harmlessness of his price policy with regard to copper may well have been difficult for Jacob Fugger to produce; the above-mentioned cartel of 1515, for instance, bound him during the period of the contract to send no Hungarian copper to Upper Germany and Italy, but rather, on threat of confiscation, to market it in the Netherlands. This agreement was obviously designed to force up the price of Tyrolese copper, upon which the Hungarian product had always had a depressing effect. And that aim itself was in the general social opinion of the time, and

[1] See Letters and Articles of Association, pp. 215 ff.

the sense of the Reichstag decrees, an attempt at "unseemly and criminal" enhancement of prices.

In view of this sharp contrast between the economico-ethical philosophy of the Reichstag and public opinion on the one hand and that of the Emperor (who was dependent on the financial resources of the merchants) and his council on the other, it is easy to understand why Jacob Fugger was not satisfied with the mandate of May 13, 1525. Political conditions at that time in Hungary and the Tyrol were more than ordinarily uncertain, which added to the necessity of a special personal imperial letter of protection referring to the two business enterprises, both of them in bad repute with the economic ethics of the time. In the movement for social reform which swept over the Tyrol in 1525, and in the nationalistic Magyar movement, which brought such heavy losses to the Fugger enterprise in its Ofen factory, and seemed to mean the end of the Fugger activity in Hungary, the charge of "usurious monopoly" was often brought against Jacob Fugger and his undertakings. In such troublous times, it was good to be well supplied with protective imperial decrees. Even though they failed at the moment when revolutionary forces took over the leadership, they were very useful when claims for compensation were being established.

It was with deep sorrow that Jacob Fugger in the.

last year of his life saw the downfall of the imposing and profitable business of the Fugger-Thurzo Company in Hungary in general and of the Fugger trading house in Ofen in particular. It was, to be sure, not entirely unexpected to this farseeing merchant. For several years, he had been very much perturbed about the Hungarian undertaking. In his first will, dating from 1521, measures were already provided for the continuance of the Fugger Company, in case of the loss of the capital invested in Hungary, which "on account of the Turks" and for other reasons "stood in grave danger."

Much more important than the Turks were the "other grounds" to which Jacob here refers, and which endangered the Fugger-Thurzo enterprise and finally produced a serious crisis. The political struggles of the various aspirants to the throne and their supporters nourished the nationalistic jealousy of the Magyars, who begrudged the foreign merchant the profits he was amassing in the land so blessed with mineral resources. These Magyar nationalists completely ignored what the Fugger-Thurzo Company accomplished for the kingdom in improving the means of transportation, increasing government revenues, raising the level of economic life, and incorporating the Hungarian mining industry into the world market—something which only a merchant of the world character of Jacob Fugger could have done. Only the dark side of the Fugger economic power in Hungary was seen, and that in exaggerated form.

The Thurzos themselves showed little capacity to alter this attitude of hostility in Hungary toward the Fugger-Thurzo enterprise. Johann, the most capable business man of the family, died in 1508, prematurely for the welfare of the Company. George, his son, weary of the Hungarian situation, and worried about the enterprise there, had moved over to Augsburg to be with the Fugger family, into which he had married. And he continued to concern himself with trifles there, in spite of all Jacob Fugger's requests that he represent the interests of the Company at the Hungarian court. His brother Alexius, on the other hand, had entered all too actively into Hungarian politics, especially into financial problems. He secured the treasurer's office, brought about an inflation through debasing the coinage, and called down the hate of the whole country upon the Fugger-Thurzo Company, to whom this debasement was without question ascribed.

Thus the whole country was against the Fuggers and the Thurzos. The leadership of the national opposition lay especially with the lower nobility, whom it was impossible to placate with presents, as the higher nobility had been. The plundering of the Ofen fac-

tory of the Fugger trading company in 1525 was at
their instigation, as was, at least in part, that of the
Neusohl factory of the Fugger-Thurzo Company.
Louis, the King, benefited by the fall of the all-too-
powerful business man, as had almost always been the
case since the downfall of the Templars and the case
of Jacques Coeur. He forced the German factor of
the Fugger Company, Alexius Thurzo, who had been
left in the lurch, to sign an agreement as a means to
self-preservation, according to which all the debts of
the King were declared canceled. Not satisfied with
that, he forced the Fugger-Thurzo representative to
renounce specifically all claims for compensation for
the plundering in Ofen and Neusohl, for the mines
in Neusohl as well as the machinery and other equipment. Further, the Company was to supply the King
with 200,000 gold gulden, of which 125,000 were to
be immediately available. In Augsburg, the enraged
Jacob Fugger dwelt on revenge and compensation.
What was to be done? Force and an appeal to justice
would be equally vain. Jacob could not even declare
null and void the agreement which had been extorted
in the name of the Company. Louis had also seized the
other Hungarian property of the Company, or had
allowed it to be seized in the territory of his uncle,
Sigmund of Poland. If Jacob disavowed the agreement publicly and at once, he could only expect

further losses. The only way which remained open to Jacob Fugger—and in this he was to be sure more fortunate than almost any other—was to bring pressure to bear upon King Louis of Hungary through powerful princely business friends, including even the Emperor. With his accustomed energy and speed, Jacob, until the last weeks of his busy life, was engaged in this process of bargaining, of requesting, of threatening, of the use of presents and of bribes. The Emperor was strongest of all in support of Jacob Fugger, notifying the King of Hungary that in case the Fuggers made an official complaint he would set the whole Empire against Hungary. This emphatic speech of the Emperor was no empty threat, if the great Augsburg merchant undertook to boycott Hungarian copper throughout Germany in case Louis did not yield.

Jacob Fugger lived to see the sun of Fugger prosperity again break slowly through the dark clouds of the East. Louis of Hungary recognized quite clearly that, without the Fuggers, the mines of his country would never achieve the highest profits. He offered a renewal of their agreement to Jacob Fugger, though it was only after the death of the great merchant that his nephews brought the transaction to a conclusion. It was Jacob, however, who laid the way for the new period of Fugger activity in Hungary, through the quiet energy and skill of his policy. This new period ran from 1526 to 1548 and saw the exclusive domination of the Fugger Company in the Hungarian field, the Thurzos having been excluded.

CHAPTER X

THE BANKER, THE EMPEROR, AND THE POPES

THERE is perhaps no other mercantile house in history—not even the House of Rothschild excepted—which so consistently and so effectively as the Fugger House employed its financial resources for its princely friends. The "grosse Politik" in Germany and Spain especially found its strongest financial support in the Fuggers. It was to Anton, the successor of Jacob the Rich in the leadership of the Fugger enterprise, that the decision fell in the matter of the Schmalkaldic War, and thus over the fate of the Reformation. And many another problem of European policy was to no less an extent decided in the Augsburg counter of these merchant princes. Even under Jacob the Rich himself, the golden threads of the Habsburg political system came together in the Fugger countingroom. In clever, often extraordinarily astute, but never incautious fashion, Jacob had developed the financial relations to the House of Habsburg which, as we have seen, his elder brother Ulrich had begun. Wherever the Habsburgs, in the last quarter of the fifteenth and the first quarter of the sixteenth centuries, attempted to extend their growing power, through negotiations or expeditions, the financial resources of the Fuggers came brilliantly to their assistance. Whether it was a question of preventing the Dukes of Bavaria from carrying out their clever plans in the Tyrol, or of putting down an uprising in the Duchy of Flanders, whether the Habsburgs used the weapons of diplomacy and of war against Charles VIII and Frances I of France, against Venice, or against the Turks, everywhere they were supported by Fugger gold and the almost inexhaustible credit of Jacob the Rich. With the help of his far-reaching trading organization, the great merchant transferred English subsidies from Antwerp to South Germany or Italy, to the leaders of the mercenary troops and the diplomats of Maximilian I. In the same way, the rich resources which Charles v controlled in Spain were concentrated quickly and certainly at the point where they were of most assistance in the achievement of the political or military aims of the Habsburgs.

When Maximilian I, the last knight, had wasted the rich resources of the Habsburg lands in a not unusually adventurous policy, when his unpaid mercenaries refused further obedience, when the imperial financial agents knew no further door on which to knock in search of additional funds, when all seemed lost for the House of Habsburg, then there still remained as a last resource the great Augsburg merchant. He did not give willingly, and he never gave without security. A transaction with this cool and clever reckoner was always difficult. But if he finally promised help, one could count absolutely on his word, and on a quick and punctual carrying out of his financial operations. Jacob had cultivated as the apple of his eye a belief in his own absolute reliability in business affairs. He always emphasized to the imperial financial agents who tried to talk him into the granting of unsecured credit, or wanted to persuade him to the granting of extensions through the promise of higher interest rates, "that he did not wish to pay off and satisfy his creditors with words, but he had to maintain his credit." As a result of his frequent transactions with the financial agents of the Crown, and with the imperial councilors, and through frequent visits of the Habsburgs and of other highly-placed persons to Augsburg, Jacob Fugger became familiar with the most secret questions of policy. His net of counters (or commercial posts), spanning all of Europe, the excellent news service which he organized and of which the highest powers often made use, the impressiveness of his gifts, which opened many otherwise silent mouths, secured to Jacob Fugger that certain knowledge of the guiding factors in the European politics of his time which enabled him to show astonishing foresight of the future distribution of power. It was no empty flattery, but a mere statement of fact, when the Council of the city of Nuremberg—for which Jacob during his life performed many services—wrote in 1519 that it did not doubt that Jacob Fugger had a very unusual knowledge of the political situation which made it possible for him to estimate with a good deal of certainty the prospects of Charles 1 of Spain in the German royal election.

There is no doubt that Jacob Fugger used his knowledge of the European political situation for his business purposes just as much as did any banker of the nineteenth or twentieth centuries, acquainted at the court or in the ministries. In the shadow of the Habsburgs, he penetrated that terrain which he, with his financial power and the assistance of his extensive mercantile organization, had helped the Habsburgs to conquer. And he knew how to pursue his own interests, along with those of the Habsburgs, in the newly-won districts. Thus it was in the Netherlands, and in Hungary and the Tyrol as well.

Nowhere better than in Hungary is it possible to observe how skillfully the great merchant used the imperialism of the Habsburgs for the carrying out of his own business aims of extension, and for bringing his own will to power. With the help of the Thurzos, Jacob Fugger was able, following in the footsteps of the Habsburgs, to establish himself in the Hungarian mining industry at the end of the fifteenth century. In spite of the hostility of the jealous Magyars, the Fugger-Thurzo Company very soon built the "common Hungarian trade" into a large and very profitable enterprise. How differently could this Fugger-Thurzo enterprise be protected from national Hungarian prejudice, as well as from the Turks, who were a constant threat, and from other hostile influences, when a Habsburg, instead of the former weak ruler, dominated the land still divided by rival parties.

How different, too, were the prospects for an unlimited market for Hungarian copper in the Empire, which was viewed by Maximilian I, who was also the Duke of the Tyrol, as the special domain of the Tyrolese products. Jacob Fugger, to be sure, in his fine diplomacy, knew how to play the economic interests of Hungary against the domination of the Tyrolese, by conveying to the Emperor through his court assistants a knowledge of how the Habsburgs would prejudice the favor which they desired from the Jagellon Vladislaw II, if they created any difficulties in the marketing of Hungary's most important article of export. But how much simpler all these things would have been, and how much more economically both Tyrolese and Hungarian copper might have found a market, if only Hungary had been in the possession of the Habsburgs!

Hence it is easy to understand why Jacob Fugger made use of all the power which he possessed to help Maximilian I in carrying to complete fruition his plans for the future of his house in eastern Europe. It was a brilliant success, not only for the House of Habsburg, but also for the Fugger House when Maximilian I at the Congress of Vienna in 1515 brought about the double marriage between his grandchildren Charles and Marie on the one hand, and Louis the son and Anna the daughter of King Vladislaw of Hungary on the other. For more than a decade, Jacob Fugger had striven to further this marriage project, and thus by strengthening the Habsburg position in Hungary to render his own position in the foreign land more secure. King Sigmund of Poland, the brother of King Vladislaw of Hungary, also appeared at the brilliant Congress of Vienna. Jacob Fugger, who wished for peace between the Emperor and Poland, which was a transit land for Hungarian copper, was energetic in his efforts to see the differences between Maximilian I and Sigmund reconciled. Jacob Fugger, accompanied by George and Alexius Thurzo, and by an imposing following, must have appeared as one of the leading participants in the success of the Habsburgs at the Congress. The bearing of the great merchant must have been like that of a prince. He distributed on all sides, to the highly-placed promoters of his business, the gold rings set with precious stones, the necklaces and pearls, and the cloths of silk, velvet, and damask which he had brought with him. No wonder that the expense account of the Fugger-Thurzo Company at the Congress of Vienna amounted to more than 10,000 Rhenish gold gulden. But Jacob Fugger knew what he was doing—in adding new and powerful friends and advocates to the old ones and in raising the reputation and credit of his House higher than ever before.

In comparison with this king of finance, how poor Maximilian 1 must have seemed to those who really understood the situation! To be sure, he appeared at the Congress with the customary splendid display, thanks to the loans previously taken up by the Fugger trading company. He and his followers wore costly decorations; their table was adorned with splendid gold and silver services. Clemens Sender, the Augsburg chronicler, a confidant of Jacob Fugger, tells us that the Emperor wished to show the foreign kings and other great princes and lords his wealth "together with that which he had in his treasuries." But those who could look behind the scene knew that Jacob Fugger was the custodian who was responsible for all these decorations and show pieces. The great merchant had, at Maximilian's request, brought them at his own risk from Augsburg, where they had been pledged with rich merchants as security for loans. Many of those who knew the real situation might well ask themselves which commanded a more real power, the Emperor who for a few days basked in the artificial splendor of these treasures, or his merchant who possessed the keys to the chests to which the pledged treasures would be returned after the ceremonies of the Congress were over. Maximilian, being a romanticist, would never have changed the appearances of his position for the realities of that of his wealthy merchant. But many of his princely contemporaries might well have been glad to do so.

To the mercantile world, and to the leading statesmen and diplomatists of the age, the full extent of Jacob Fugger's power was most clearly shown by the assistance which he rendered to the House of Habsburg when the problem arose of securing the emperorship for the grandchild of Maximilian I, that is, King Charles I of Spain, who later became Emperor Charles V. It was, perhaps, the most important question in the European politics of the age whether Francis I should add the German royal and imperial crown to his French one, or whether the Habsburgs should be the protectors of the Holy Roman Empire. While the money and credit of the Fuggers did not actually bring about the decision, certainly they did much to make sure that the Habsburgs were able to put greater weight in their side of the scale.

The struggle between Francis I of France and Charles I of Spain over the succession began in the last years of the reign of Maximilian I. Francis sought the support of the Electors with every possible sacrifice. If Maximilian I and Charles I of Spain were unable to command as large sums as those of the House of Valois, it was impossible for the Habsburgs to count upon the votes of the Electors of Mainz and of Trier, of the Count Palatine of the Rhine, and of the Margrave Joachim of Brandenburg. To be sure, Maximilian I in 1518, at the Augsburg Reichstag, under the eyes, so to speak, of Jacob Fugger, and supported by his financial resources, did succeed in winning the Electors and their councils for his grandson. Only the Elector of Saxony made reservations. But it would have been self-deception to conclude from this that the election of the Spanish Habsburgs was assured. There were still many difficult arrangements to be made. Before the goal was reached, large sums of money had still to be sacrificed, in addition to those paid out or promised at Augsburg in 1518.

Jacob Fugger played his most important part in the dealings with the Elector of Brandenburg. Francis I had promised the Elector's son a French wife with a rich dowry, in case he voted for the French King. Maximilian 1 outbid his opponent by promising the son of Joachim of Brandenburg the hand of his grand-daughter, a sister of Charles 1 of Spain, together with a marriage portion of about 300,000 Rhenish gold gulden. The Fugger Company bound itself, in an agreement signed by Jacob and his nephews Raimund and Ulrich, to turn over to the Elector 100,000 Rhenish gold gulden immediately after the election. The contract was not carried out, for the death of Maximilian, with the delay which it brought in the election, created a new situation and new difficulties for the Habsburgs. The Electors, continually urged by Francis 1, again wavered in their decision. The greedy Brandenburger in particular could not decide whether to throw in his fortunes with the House of Habsburg or with that of Valois.

In addition, Charles 1 made the mistake of not relying on Jacob Fugger, as Maximilian 1 had done, as his chief aide in the financial transactions connected with the election. Charles depended more for the transfer to Germany of the election funds already raised and still to be raised in his Iberian kingdom, on the Augsburg firm Anton Welser and Company, which was better known in Spain, as well as on several Genoese banking houses. Jacob Fugger was commissioned by the envoy of Charles I of Spain at the beginning of the year 1519 only to take over in deposit the specified amount of exchange. The amounts concerned were considerable, as can be seen from the fact that the Spanish factors of Anton Welser and Company alone transferred sums amounting to 143,333 Rhenish gold gulden to the Welser representative in Frankfurt on the Main, where the election was to be held, while three Italians, especially Genoese, firms operating in Spain wished to transfer a total of 165,000 Rhenish gold gulden through Frankfurt on the Main.

With anger in his heart, Jacob Fugger acknowledged the receipt of the letters of exchange, and placed them, in accordance with the wishes of the Spanish monarch, for safe-keeping in the secure chests of his golden countingroom. It angered the mighty man, who rightly considered himself indispensable to the House of Habsburg, to lose an easy profit in this Spanish exchange, a relatively secure undertaking. It appeared likely that he would have to take over the later exchange and loans, involving much more risk, when, as appeared most likely to occur, the Spanish resources were exhausted. For Jacob neither would nor could sacrifice a leading part in the most important political and financial transaction of his generation. He knew too well the business advantages

which had come to him directly and especially indirectly as a result of his activity as court banker
under Maximilian I. To allow himself to be driven
out now by the Welsers would be too ominous for
the business future of the House of Fugger. Perhaps
also that strong feeling of power which arose out of
business relations with the foremost power of Christendom had become indispensable to Jacob. The
great financier did not lack friends who would help
him to return to a leading position in the Spanish
business, nor courtiers who would apprise Charles I
of the importance of Jacob Fugger to his election
prospects. He himself, in order to achieve his purpose,
did not hesitate to acquaint Charles I with the services which his firm had performed for the House of
Habsburg, nor with its brilliant prospects in case it
transferred its support to the ambitious plans of
Francis I. The Electors of the Holy Roman Empire
proposed that Jacob conduct the great financial transactions, into which the election of Charles I had partly
resolved itself. Only the mercantile reputation of
Jacob the Rich gave the necessary assurance to their
greed for money that the financial promises preceding the election would and could be fully realized
after the election in the gold gulden which alone
would satisfy the Electors. And so the Elector of
Mainz proposed to cancel the pledges of the rich cities.

of Antwerp and Mechlin, and to substitute for them
Jacob Fugger's pledge. The other Electors, especially
Joachim of Brandenburg, were similarly disposed.
They were unwilling to accept assurances for their
money from anyone else, even from the Welsers. And
thus Jacob Fugger finally returned to the leadership
of the financial transactions which were connected
with the imperial election. Especially in the second;
decisive stage of the dealings with the Electors, the
great merchant prince of Augsburg extended credit
to King Charles I to the extent of considerably more
than half a million Rhenish gold gulden, more than
three times as much as all the Italians referred to
above put together, and almost four times as much
as the Welsers had extended.

Notwithstanding this great achievement, Jacob
Fugger did not fully accomplish his aim, which was
from the beginning to monopolize the whole trans-
action, and to exclude all competition completely.
Charles I, to be sure, after he recognized the error
in his former policy toward the Fuggers, agreed en-
tirely with the injured merchant and his demands.
But the Genoese competitors, as well as the Welsers,
wished to save their faces as against the victorious
Fugger, and to preserve their mercantile reputations.
The Italians steadfastly opposed all attempts of
Charles I to secure their agreement to realize on their

exchange at once and to place the money in the hands of the Fuggers; or even to pledge the Fuggers that the money would be paid to them when the exchange fell due. Let the despised Fugger find the covering for the security which he was to give the Electors where he might; they refused to put either money or pledge in his hands. Not for any price nor for any advantage—so they expressed themselves to the representatives of Charles—would they subordinate themselves to the Fuggers in this matter. They could not do it for their honor's sake, and they would not do it on account of the lack of consideration and the many injuries to their credit of which Jacob Fugger had been guilty.

It was a prolonged and severe battle in European high finance which was here played out alongside the struggle between the Habsburgs and the Valois over the imperial throne. In vain the Welsers declared themselves prepared to offer pledges for their exchange and that of the Italians, independently of the Fuggers, thus furnishing security to the Electors. The latter continued in their position that they would deal only with Jacob Fugger.

Thus the great Augsburger eventually emerged victor from this competition of the bankers. The Habsburgs had him chiefly to thank that on June 28, 1519, Charles 1 of Spain was elected King of Germany. They were not, however, and Charles v in particular was not in any haste to show Jacob Fugger his gratitude by prompt repayment of the debt which had assumed immense proportions. The redemption took place only very slowly, and not infrequently new demands for money from the Augsburg banker were substituted for payments. On one such occasion at the beginning of the year 1523, Jacob Fugger wrote that famous letter to Charles v, the chief part of which, in somewhat modernized diction, reads about as follows:

His Most Serene, All-Powerful Roman Emperor,
and Most Gracious Lord!

Your Royal Majesty is undoubtedly well aware of the extent to which I and my nephews have always been inclined to serve the House of Austria, and in all submissiveness to promote its welfare and its rise. For that reason, we co-operated with the former Emperor Maximilian, Your Imperial Majesty's forefather, and, in loyal subjection to His Majesty, to secure the Imperial Crown for Your Imperial Majesty, pledged ourselves to several princes, who placed their confidence and trust in me as perhaps in no one else. We also, when Your Imperial Majesty's appointed delegates were treating for the completion of the above-mentioned undertaking, furnished a considerable sum of money which was secured, not from me and my nephews alone, but from some of my good friends at heavy cost, so that the excellent nobles achieved success to the great honor and well-being of Your Imperial Majesty.

It is also well known that Your Majesty without me might not have acquired the Imperial Crown, as I can attest with the written statement of all the delegates of Your Imperial Majesty. And in all this I have looked not to my own profit. For if I had withdrawn my support from the House of Austria, and transferred it to France, I should have won large profit and much money, which were at that time offered to me. But what disadvantage would have risen thereby for the House of Austria, Your Imperial Majesty with your deep comprehension may well conceive.

Taking all this into consideration, my respectful request to Your Imperial Majesty is that you will graciously recognize my faithful, humble service, dedicated to the greater well-being of Your Imperial Majesty, and that you will order that the money which I have paid out, together with the interest upon it, shall be reckoned up and paid, without further delay. In order to deserve that from Your Imperial Majesty, I pledge myself to be faithful in all humility, and I hereby commend myself as faithful at all times to Your Imperial Majesty.

Your Imperial Majesty's most humble servant

JACOB FUGGER

What Jacob Fugger wrote here to Charles v, the mightiest ruler of the earth, the Emperor on whose domains the sun never sank, was true, though it must have been bitter truth for the pride of the Habsburgs. But these words were also written by an All-Powerful—these firm sentences, ringing with justifiable pride, which will always remain one of the most interesting pages in the annals of German mercantile greatness.

Toward Maximilian I, Jacob Fugger could never have used such self-assertive language. It was only after Maximilian's death, in the financial and political struggles and deals which were bound up with the election of Charles v, that Jacob Fugger rose to that measure of greatness which made him the declared leader of his contemporaries. From the time that he, in full knowledge of the political situation, and in clear recognition of the business consequences of his conduct, made himself, almost by force one might say, the leading banker of Charles v, his position of leadership in European high finance could no longer be questioned. In vain had Bartholomew Welser, the ablest member of this family, which, next to that of the Fuggers, was the greatest mercantile family of Germany, attempted to exploit his excellent Spanish connections—which were, indeed, better than those of Jacob Fugger—in order to come at one step into close business relations with the Habsburgs, and to deprive Jacob Fugger of the exclusive position which he had acquired under Maximilian I. In vain also had the Italian, particularly the Genoese bankers, who were active in Spain sought to break into the financial affairs of the Holy Roman Empire by way of the election business with the presumptive German king. Jacob Fugger destroyed all such prospects of competition. Under the astonished eyes of the European banking world, he established himself more firmly than ever in the saddle with the Habsburgs. From that time onward, his reputation in the international mercantile world was extraordinary. It was not an exaggeration when Clemens Sender, the Augsburg chronicler, in proud admiration of the man whom he knew personally, made the claim that the name of Jacob Fugger and his brothers' sons was known in all lands and kingdoms, even in the pagan world. Emperors, kings, princes, and lords sent their ambassadors to him. All the merchants of the world looked upon him as an illustrious man, and the heathen admired him. He became a credit to the whole German land.

During the last five years of his life, Jacob Fugger's business reputation was unique. His credit knew no bounds. Even before his death, legends began to cluster about his person and his wealth. We find the first traces with Luther, for even this reformer, who on social and religious grounds was hostile toward Jacob Fugger, revealed a certain degree of pride in the fact that this mightiest merchant of his time was a German. In one of his table-talks, he attributed to the pope the words spoken to the cardinals of France and England: would their kings be able to collect three tons of gold in an hour. When they said no, the pope retorted that a citizen of Augsburg could do so.

Perhaps the opinion of Jacob Fugger in Rome was not so high as this. But it was great enough, even after discounting such fabulous exaggerations. At the time of Jacob's death, the Papal See had been carrying on for more than a generation various and ever increasing business relations with the Fugger trading house. The goods trade played a minor rôle here, although the papacy not infrequently secured supplies of metals from the Fuggers, especially silver for its mints, copper, lead, and zinc for its arsenals and munitions factories, etc. But on the whole, the goods trade was of subordinate importance, the financial relations undoubtedly occupying the foreground. The Fuggers, however, created nothing new of fundamental importance in the history of papal finance. Rather, they continued a system, alongside and in addition to the Italian high finance, which in its essentials had been worked out about three centuries before, and the main lines of which were sketched above.

The business which the Fugger trading company had carried on with the Papal See under Ulrich's leadership—following in the footsteps of other South German merchants—had been sporadic, and for the most part remained so. It was only after Jacob had. more and more taken over the direction of the Company that the business with Rome increased in importance. Jacob Fugger succeeded in doing what no other German or French merchant had been able to do—that is, to become in large measure the banker of the papacy. In doing so, he exceeded even those most important financiers of the popes, the Medici, at least as far as the geographical extent of his business was concerned. The Fugger House exercised a rapidly growing influence upon papal finance from about the year 1495. Jacob Fugger soon succeeded in taking away from the other European bankers, especially the Italians, the business of the Papal See in Germany, as well as in Scandinavia and the Slavic and

Magyar lands. About the year 1495, the payments of the dues of the upper and lower Church dignitaries of northern and eastern Europe to the papal treasury began to be made regularly through the Augsburg banking house and its branches. By this year, there was a branch of the Company in Rome, which at least until the year 1527 played a rôle of increasing importance among the banking houses of the Eternal City.

By the end of the pontificate of Alexander VI (1503), the Fugger family partnership was already acting as intermediary for most of the receipts of the See from Hungary, Poland, and Germany, though not from the Netherlands. The higher clergy of the Scandinavian lands also turned to the Fuggers, especially when there were dues of various sorts to be transferred to Rome. Jacob even achieved a complete monopoly in the financial relations of the Papal See to Germany. From 1515–20 until the death of Jacob, it was an exception when the spiritual princes transferred their payments to Rome through other hands than those of the Fuggers. The profits of the Fugger House were large and comparatively certain and easy on this transfer business and the loans connected with it to those who had not the money at hand to make the payments demanded from Rome. A special source of profit were the interest payments, to which, in spite of the theoretical maintenance of the canonical prohibition of interest, the papacy and clergy had had to submit for centuries, in order to carry out the world organization of the Church. Nevertheless it was an exaggeration when the Cardinal Luigi d'Aragona, who came to Jacob Fugger's hospitable house as a result of a northern journey in 1517, wrote in his diary that the chief source of the wealth of the Fuggers was the loans to those "who have to make payments to Rome for appointments to bishoprics, abbotships, and great benefices."

Against the profits from such business often stood heavy losses in the case of the higher clergy, to whom Fugger advanced their payments to the papacy. And not infrequently the financial relations with the See made it necessary for the German merchant to extend credit to the extravagant popes of the Renaissance period, credit which was secured in part and not too soundly by the receipts of the Papal See in northern Europe or elsewhere. In the Fugger inventory of the year 1527, rather large debts of Leo x are listed among the irrecoverable assets of the Roman branch of the firm. They had arisen out of advances of money for luxuries and for purposes of representation (the fitting out of papal legates and nuncios with the necessary financial resources), and especially for purposes of war. The financing of the papal army and its Swiss soldiers consumed large sums, which often had to be supplied by Jacob Fugger.

It was thus not without risk that Fugger had secured his position of power in the inner administration of the Church, the extraordinary character of which is perhaps best indicated by a remark made by the Augsburg merchant to Cardinal Luigi d'Aragona, boasting that "he had been concerned in the appointment of all the German bishops; often indeed two or three times." Not infrequently this co-operation took place without regard to the precepts of the Church, which strongly criticized as simony the acquisition of spiritual goods and offices through the use of gold or valuables. The financial organization which Fugger had built up in the business transactions with the Papal See indeed favored the concentration of spiritual offices in the hands of one person, and the simonistic trafficking in benefices indulged in by clergy who forgot their responsibilities. The German seekers after benefices now had a strong support in Rome in the financial power of the Fuggers. There is no doubt, according to the reliable and unbiased researches of Aloys Schulte,[1] that, for example, the accumulation of three bishoprics upon the shoulders of Albrecht of Brandenburg, and the simony connected with it, which was initiated by the papal office, the Dataria,

[1] *Die Fugger in Rom, 1495–1523*, 2 vols. (Leipzig, 1904).

was accepted by the papacy, and financed by the Fuggers, would have been impossible except for the financial resources of the German trading house. There is no doubt also that the Roman factor of the Fuggers, the cleric Johannes Zink, treated the benefices which he had secured through Fugger influence as a commodity.

This German cleric, Johannes Zink, was just as. guilty as his Roman contemporaries of the malpractices so common to these spiritual courtiers of a worldly papacy. And it was Fugger gold that furnished him the necessary means. A dark shadow thus falls on Jacob Fugger as well. It is not fair, to be sure, to demand of him that he be more spiritual than the worldly popes, that he refrain from carrying on deals which the Italian bankers had not hesitated to carry on before him. But the responsibility for making known and spreading all these malpractices in Germany, where they were laid at the door of the papacy itself, and not, as in Italy, ascribed to human frailty and lusts; and the responsibility for the schism which grew partly, though of course not wholly, out of this must in the last analysis be laid partly on the shoulders of the great Augsburg merchant.

From about the year 1502, the Fugger open trading company also began to carry on an intensive business in the transfer from Germany to Rome of the money arising out of fees for indulgences. Here, also, Jacob Fugger achieved a profitable monopoly. His representatives took in charge that part of the proceeds of the indulgences which belonged to the See. The central office in Augsburg then transferred the money to Rome, or canceled it off against debts there. This participation in the business of indulgences also drew down on Jacob Fugger a part of that deep hostility felt in wide circles in Germany against the abuses of many of those who preached indulgences. How passionately Luther and Ulrich von Hutten attacked the business of the Fuggers connected with the indulgences, and their financial relations with the See in general. Every misuse of indulgences, every case of simony, every unworthy sale of a benefice seemed to these two, and to thousands of other more objectively-minded Germans, to find its financial basis in the Augsburg trading house. These were, to be sure, for the most part unjustified attacks. It was of course not fair to make the merchant responsible for the unjust outgrowths of the trade in indulgences; he was obviously unable to examine the origins of the money which he was to tranfer to Rome. But was Jacob Fugger not involved in the granting of that questionable indulgence to Albrecht of Brandenburg, which was ostensibly connected with the construction of Saint Peter's, but the actual purpose of which was to facilitate for this greatest of German seekers after benefices the raising of the necessary funds for simony and the accumulation of bishoprics? Was not this indulgence the immediate cause which led to Luther's turn against the Church?

It was exactly this economic objection, which almost all Germans made against indulgences—even when they were free of all questionable associations—that led to the sharpest attacks on the Fuggers. From the economic point of view, the following strong objection could be levied against the indulgence, even when it was used in accordance with the purpose of the Church, without any abuse. As a result of the large share of the See in the proceeds of the indulgences ($33\frac{1}{3}$ to 50 per cent), it was looked upon as bringing about a very dangerous export of gold from Germany. This amounted to a bleeding of German economic life, all the more undesirable as other states, including Spain, France, and even England, had strictly protected themselves against such losses.

So long as the territorial princes, who participated heavily in the proceeds of the indulgences, had not the strength to follow the example of the states named above, the Papal See could have allowed its financial affairs in Germany to be handled by Italian bankers. But the Papal See knew what it was doing when it gave its business to a German house with its representatives in Germany and in northern and eastern Europe generally. The Fuggers knew the northern ground and its financial possibilities far better than, for instance, did the Medici.

From his exchange business, Jacob Fugger penetrated the internal administration of the Church. He played, for instance, an important part in the history of the papal coinage system. Not that the German banker, like earlier Italian houses, achieved a monopoly in this field. In many of the papal mints, the Fuggers were of no importance, except as they supplied silver from Hungary or the Tyrol. But coinage in Rome from toward the end of the pontificate of Julius II until the time of Clement VII, that is, from about 1510 until 1534, was essentially the domain of the Fuggers. Even today, the more important coin collections in Europe contain papal coins of this time, which bear the Fugger trade-mark, the famous trident or an F rising out of a ring. Until the researches of Aloys Schulte, these marks were unintelligible to the numismatists. Now they furnish us the proof that the great German merchant occupied an outstanding position in the field of papal coinage.

The business consequences of the relations of the Fuggers with the papacy were by no means so important, but were at least much more profitable than those with the emperors. It was a blessing for the

German merchant that he carried on so skilfully the business of Leo x especially, that brilliant, but exceedingly extravagant Medicean pope. A wicked, but very appropriate witticism circulated in Rome after the death of Leo x, to the effect that this Pope had spent the funds of three pontificates, the surplus of Julius ii, the receipts during his own administration, and those of his successor, to whom he left a heavy burden of debt. In such a state of affairs, the sum of about 15,000 Roman ducats, carried in the Fugger inventory of 1527 as a papal debt from the time of Leo x, seems very moderate. In addition, it was at least partly secured by a costly ring, pledged by the Pope. How much more extensive sums had Jacob Fugger found it necessary to loan to the kings and emperors of the House of Habsburg, to be sure not without security, but in debts that were realized only very slowly! The business of Jacob Fugger with the emperors greatly exceeded that with the popes in any case. Not in the southern Italian skies, but in the northern and western Spanish skies, the politico-financial background of the later Fugger generations was to become overcast with those dark clouds which concealed the catastrophe which was to overtake the Fugger House.

CHAPTER XI

JACOB FUGGER AS HIS CONTEMPORARIES SAW HIM. HIS CHARITABLE ENDOWMENTS

I⊤ is easy to understand that so striking a personality as Jacob Fugger aroused a good deal of interest among his contemporaries, and, according to their views, provoked either active hostility or excessive admiration. On the whole, there can be no doubt that the opposition aroused by his activity was stronger and more prevalent than the approval. This opposition began among his own merchant colleagues. How marked, for instance, was the hostility of the Genoese financiers to the man who had outranked them in the financial transactions connected with the election of Charles v! And the Welsers, on the same grounds, entirely agreed with the adverse criticism of the Italian bankers. Frequently, too, in the competition of the German merchants for leadership in the various spice contracts with the Portuguese Crown, Jacob Fugger and his representatives were accused of lack of consideration and a complete neglect of the common interests of the German merchants active abroad.

It is impossible to ascertain now what measure of truth these accusations contained.

In any case, we need not take such complaints too seriously. When there was an opportunity of supplanting a competitor in the control of a rich source of profit, other merchants, under even worse circumstances, also forgot the common interests of the Germans; indeed, they did what Jacob Fugger never did —they forgot the national dignity. In the year 1525, for instance, the Nuremberg merchants, supported by the city Council, hastened to take charge of the Hungarian mining from which the Fugger-Thurzo Company had been driven under such ignominious circumstances by the national Hungarian party.

A strong modern entrepreneurship like that of Jacob Fugger, which reached out into all fields, met with conflict even in the circles of the Hanseatic merchants, with their emphasis upon outlived privileges and their exclusion of all non-Hanseatics from their extended eastern and northern European trading districts. One can understand the hostility of the conservative Hanseatic merchants, who only too willingly opposed any progressive competition with their rights of exclusion, when it is recognized that Jacob Fugger ignored the right of staple which the Hanse had established for Bruges, and dispatched his large copper shipments from Danzig and Stettin only to the free port of the rapidly growing Antwerp; that he followed a policy which differed from that of the Hanse in its relations with the king of Denmark, on account of the fees for passage of the Sound, and with the king of Sweden on account of the Swedish copper mines; and that he threatened the mercantile domination of the Hanseatic League right to the furthest corner of the Baltic Sea region, to Novgorod in northern Russia.

Elsewhere also we see Jacob Fugger, like other merchants of his stamp, in conflict with the traditional authorities in control of trade, and involved in many dissensions. The lesser merchants—today we would call them the middle class—were engaged in a struggle against the great trading companies and their attempts at monopoly and their formation of cartels, and against their increasing tendency to establish networks of branches. This struggle naturally expressed itself most strongly in hostility to Jacob Fugger, who was the leader of the modern commercial entrepreneurship. When there was discussion in the Reichstag or in the provincial legislatures of this tendency to eliminate the smaller merchants or of the injuries to the interests of the consumers caused by the concentration of capital, no other name was mentioned so often as that of Jacob Fugger. Indeed, the Fugger trading company, even in the first decades of the sixteenth century, was considered so typical of the great companies that in the Württemberg legislature, the companies were designated as "Fuggers." And soon in Swabia as well, the expression "to fugger" meant to carry on trade in general, and in the popular mind it had an evil connotation in the sense of usurious trade or sharp practices.

Other levels of society found themselves in agreement with the threatened merchant class in its judgment of the business principles and the forms of organization of trade represented by Jacob Fugger. The upper nobility, deprived of its former significance in the political and cultural life of the nation, and the lower nobility, impoverished and uneducated, found themselves more and more excluded from the influential positions in Church and state by the sons of rich merchant families, and both saw in Jacob Fugger the leading factor in their social decline. Ulrich von Hutten, the spokesman of the nobility, hated this greatest of tradesmen, against whom he had also a religious feeling, since he realized what a support Jacob Fugger was to the old religion, and how indispensable he was to the Papal See as a financier. Jacob Fugger must have clearly recognized the hostility commonly felt toward him in the ranks of nobility when he acquired, in addition to other feudal landed possessions, the domain of Kirchberg. The

Duke of Württemberg and the Count of Zollern both tried to wrest away from him these legally acquired domains, and the lesser noble at least showed his hostility to the merchant by refusing to recognize the suzerainty of Jacob Fugger in his newly acquired domains, and would not consider himself a vassal of this commoner who had accumulated wealth. In order to deal sharply with such insubordination, Jacob Fugger accepted the rank of nobility from the Emperor in 1511 and the title of Count in 1514.

A considerable part of the hostility to Jacob Fugger evident in contemporary society rested without doubt upon dislike and envy. To many, it was unbearable that one man should concentrate so much financial power in a fashion hitherto unknown. Jacob Fugger certainly understood them when he wrote to Duke George of Saxony: "Many in the world are hostile toward me. They say I am rich. I am rich by God's grace, without injury to any man." Even social theorists of the time, those of the Catholic or the Lutheran faith preaching economic ethics, attacked Fugger's economic principles and his business practices, especially his formation of cartels and his monopolistic tendencies, and made him responsible for all the increases in the prices of metals, spices, etc. They were actuated by much higher motives than the envious, but they went much too far in their attacks and their hostility. Those who investigate the causes of the rise of prices in the sixteenth century know that the decisive factor was not the eagerness of the merchants in their search for profits, though that eagerness was certainly great. The tendency toward monopoly and the formation of cartels in the ore trade of the sixteenth century had a strong economic basis, which Charles v stated clearly in the bill of May 13, 1525, mentioned above,[1] which was undoubtedly inspired chiefly by Jacob Fugger, and which declared monopoly in the mining industry to be legal. For there could be no doubt in the minds of those who really understood the situation at that time, however small their numbers might be, that this most important branch of German economic life could expand only if aided by modern measures and modern points of view. The only possible way of continuing and increasing the investment of capital in mining, to the benefit of the whole German economic system, was to ensure to that capital—and this was the basic principle of the bill— a high return, and one as regular as possible, in order to compensate for the risk involved. Monopoly alone provided such a return. The bill in astute fashion especially defended monopoly as a protection against those injuries which a great variation in the price of mining products and the withdrawal of capital from

[1] See above, p. 132.

unprofitable mines would work upon the laboring population concerned.

There are other factors than the economic one, a proper understanding of which enables us to examine more objectively than could his contemporary attackers—who generally lacked understanding of the economic situation—the charges of monopoly against Jacob Fugger. In the sixteenth-century evolution of capitalism, the lords played a rôle of no less importance than the merchants in the development of monopoly. And the state, as we saw above,[1] on account of its financial needs, stood godfather to the modern forms of capitalistic organization. The Council of the city of Augsburg was entirely right when in its memorial to the Reichstag it maintained that monopolies were formed not alone by great merchants, indeed, their development was due in greater degree to princes, who were the promoters and sellers of many monopolies.

Finally, in order to judge Jacob Fugger's conduct fairly, it is necessary to remember that, although the prices of ore, spices, and other monopolized products went up rapidly in the course of the sixteenth century, the chief responsibility does not lie with the entrepreneurs. The princes, who could establish monopolies through the use of their royal prerogative,

[1] See above, p. 46.

gradually increased to a very high point the share of
the state in the monopoly profits. They did this largely
through their skilled financial agents and court councilors, who generally offered a monopoly which was
to be granted to a number of merchants at the same
time. Then followed a well-known and deliberate
competition, which was in the interest of the princely
finances. It was when one entrepreneur could be
played off against another that the royal treasury
came out best, as the merchants bid against one another. But the result was that the price of the commodity involved had to be forced up by the entrepreneur, if he were to regain his expenditures. Thus,
behind Jacob Fugger in his attempts at monopoly
stood the needy princes of his time, as inciters—promoters, we call them in modern economic terminology. And the objective critic must place on the latter
at least a part of the blame for the increase of prices
which in the sixteenth century was attributed to
Jacob Fugger and his contemporaries alone. Jacob
Fugger was limited, as all men are, by the existing
conditions which he did not create; he could not have
freed himself from them even had he wished to. That
he was not in reality the unconditional monopolist,
the brutal man of force, which his prejudiced contemporaries saw in him is sufficiently proved by his
well-known benevolence, and by his numerous en-

dowments for the poor, the weak, and the ill. Indeed, it is these evidences of his social point of view that have created for the prince of wealth his most lasting, as well as his clearest and most uncontested, memorial in history. Like other rich merchants of the late medieval period, Jacob Fugger expressed his benevolence in numerous generous endowments for religious purposes and for the poor. In one endowment, however, he broke a new path. This was the establishment of the so-called Fuggerei in Augsburg. In order to combat the lack of homes for poor day laborers and handworkers, Jacob Fugger had constructed at the edge of the city a sort of garden city, as we would call it today. He thus solved the dwelling problem in the happiest fashion for more than a hundred families, by the more than fifty attractive cottages, each of which housed two families, at a nominal rent. This center, the first small-house colony, still exists today, well cared for and protected, surrounded by a special wall, and provided with its own church, like a little world of its own in the midst of the city—for the city has now, of course, grown up around it. Even today, it adds to the welfare of hundreds, is one of the sights of Augsburg, and is without doubt one of the most lasting achievements of the Augsburg merchant prince. How much importance Jacob Fugger laid on the Fuggerei, this greatest of his benefactions, can be judged from the fact that in his will, a few days before his death, he remembered the inhabitants of this colony, and left to each family with children a Rhenish gold gulden; to each family without children, half a Rhenish gold gulden.

Whatever may be thought of the great entrepreneur and business leader who died four hundred years ago, his establishment of the Fuggerei won him permanent fame. In this, and in his other charitable undertakings, Jacob Fugger looked beyond the cares of his own business and the future of the family, into the realm of general social well-being. This is well expressed in the Latin inscription over the chief entrance to the Fuggerei, which commemorates the donor and his deed:

1519

Ulrich, George, and Jacob Fugger of Augsburg, blood brothers, being firmly convinced that they were born for the good of the city, and that for their great property they have to thank chiefly an all-powerful and benevolent God, have out of piety, and as an example of special generosity founded, given, and dedicated 106 dwellings, both buildings and furnishings, to those of their fellow citizens who live righteously, but are beset by poverty.

A View of the Fuggerei, in Augsburg

CHAPTER XII

JACOB FUGGER'S MERCANTILE CHARACTER.
THE SECRET OF HIS SUCCESS. HIS DEATH

THE outward appearance of Jacob Fugger is well known to us, thanks to the various portrait commissions which the wealthy patron of art gave to the greatest German artists of his time, Albrecht Dürer, Hans Burgkmair, Hans Holbein the Elder, and Schwarz. But we are not so fortunate in our knowledge of his temperament. The direct sources furnish us almost no information. There is no private, and no extensive business correspondence to give us insight into the ideas and emotions of this great man. The immediate source material gives us very little knowledge even of his business principles and aims, his characteristic intellectual resources, and all those factors which help to account for his brilliant career. We are forced to rely almost entirely upon inferences from his conduct itself to penetrate the darkness which surrounds the secret of his unparalleled business success.

We cited above [1] a few figures—very impressive ones, to be sure—which indicated the boundaries of

---

[1] See above, pp. 86–89.

Fugger's mercantile activity as they expanded from year to year. From these figures alone, and the rapidity with which they grow, an impression can be gained of the rare good fortune which was his lot, the success of his speculative undertakings, the rich returns gained from fortunate business deals. But to the more critical observer, it is clear that it was not romantic accident, but regular industrious labor from day to day which constituted the basis of Fugger's unusual achievement. As an apprentice and young man, Jacob Fugger shrank from none of the hardships of his mercantile calling. This highly educated son of an old and wealthy merchant house lived for weeks together in the deep forests of Thuringia, shut off like a charcoal-burner from all civilization, in order to supervise the construction of the Fugger-Thurzo smelting works and the equipment of the plant. This was typical of the unwearying activity of his whole life. For weeks and months together he traveled, visiting the fairs, supervising the branches, watching the business himself, carrying out the difficult transactions with the councilors and the financial agents of the Habsburgs. Even as he aged, he seemed to suffer no exhaustion, no loss of joy in his work. When clouds gathered on the Hungarian sky of the Fugger-Thurzo Company, and a member of the Thurzo family advised him to liquidate the business there and to leave the dangerous field to someone else, the inexhaustible old man looked on such an attitude as pusillanimous, and replied with the words already cited in another connection: "He was of quite a different point of view; and wished to continue making a profit as long as he could."

Excellent health, which did not forsake him even in his older years, up to the last days of his life, gave Jacob Fugger the necessary strength for such energy. He knew nothing of nervousness during his whole life. In the evening, he laid the cares of the day aside, and the next morning put his hand afresh to the plow. One of the members of the family tells us that he laid all the cares of the business away with his clothes before he went to sleep at night.

With his industry, Jacob Fugger combined a great talent for trade, a sure sense of business. He clearly recognized the overwhelming importance of mining and the trade in ore for South German business in his day, and acted accordingly. He shrank from no exertion, no difficulty necessary for the development and large-scale exploitation of this field of early capitalistic entrepreneurship. And there were great difficulties to be overcome in Hungary before production was on its feet and the marketing had been turned into the proper channels. Aside from all the political obstacles, serious technical difficulties had to be solved. Smelting works had to be erected, streams regulated, long roads built, before the transportation of the ore produced could be successfully carried out, and the metals of the East European Carpathians could become a product of world trade.

It is, in fact, just here in Hungary that Jacob Fugger's activity and power assume large proportions, almost Faustian, one might say, had this expression not become somewhat discredited through overcommon usage by modern authors. It is here in Hungary that the creative greatness of an entrepreneur like Jacob Fugger, whose activity and achievements are manifold, comes most clearly to expression:

The night seems deeper now to press around me,
But in my inmost spirit all is light;
I rest not till the finished work hath crowned me:
The master's word alone bestows the might.
Up from your couches, vassals, man by man!
Make grandly visible my daring plan!

Seize now your tools, with spade and shovel press!
The work traced out must be a swift success.
Quick diligence, severest ordering
The most superb reward shall bring;
And, that the mighty work completed stands,
One mind suffices for a thousand hands.[1]

---

[1] Johann Wolfgang von Goethe, *Faust*, Part II, Act v, Scene v. Translated in the original metres by Bayard Taylor (Boston, 1887).

Jacob Fugger's talent for organization not only broke new paths in the development of trade, but exploited for the benefit of his enterprises the whole machinery for the communication of news. That same auxiliary which was in the nineteenth century to aid the Rothschilds in the achievement of their great business success, the securing of rapid and reliable information concerning all those events which can be of use to the merchant, was developed by Jacob Fugger with no less skill three hundred years earlier. Like the nineteenth-century Frankfurt bankers, Fugger had a well-developed and reliable courier service, which at once brought all news of important political and economic events to headquarters at Augsburg. Like the Rothschilds, too, and apparently even more extensively than they, he had connections at the courts and in the state chancelleries, which furnished him with information concerning political affairs such as no other merchant possessed or could make use of.

Jacob Fugger also utilized the practice of his time of securing "news," that is, information concerning political and other events, through the exchange of letters with correspondents of both princely and bourgeois rank. Such news came to his Augsburg countingroom with every post, along with the actual trade correspondence. Information of this kind was also sent by agents of high or low rank at the princely courts, who were paid or were won over by rich gifts. The harmless news, and that which was not valuable, or was no longer valuable, from a business point of view, Jacob Fugger then passed on to his correspondents. To that part which was important for his mercantile transactions, however, he clung with the secrecy which characterized the clever business man then as now. His nephew Anton undoubtedly owed one of his business principles: "Silence is the thing" to the influence and experience of his great master and uncle.

.   .   .   .

When in December of the year 1525, the German King Ferdinand on the occasion of a session of the provincial legislature entered Augsburg in official procession, the King's trumpeters and kettle-drummers were ordered to silence as the head of the procession neared the Fugger house. Clemens Sender, the Augsburg chronicler, tells us that the Habsburger with all his train passed in complete silence the palace in which Jacob Fugger lay dying.

On December 30 of that year, Jacob Fugger died without issue in his splendid house am Weinmarkt. Anton, his nephew, took over the leadership of the business. And it was under him, building upon the firm foundations which Jacob the Rich had laid, that the Fugger trading company reached the culmination of its strength, and of its mercantile, industrial, and financial accomplishments. In the year 1546, at the height of its development, the business property of the firm reached almost 5,000,000 gold gulden. Under Anton, too, who controlled the Company until his death in 1560, the outward power and the European reputation of the firm was not less than it had been under his great uncle. The policies of the German and Spanish Habsburgs, and of other princes, found a strong support in his financial capacity, as they had earlier in that of Jacob the Rich. Anton Fugger was the leading merchant of his time, as was granted by the best informed among his contemporaries. Even the Italian competitors were full of admiration for this prince of merchants in Augsburg. But the strength and solidity which the Fugger Company had possessed under Jacob the Rich was lost about the middle of the sixteenth century. Anton was not so outstanding an entrepreneur as his gifted uncle. As time went on, he was unable to stem the flood of loans to the Habsburgs, and unable also to compensate for the losses in that sphere by the expansion of trade and increased profits there. Anton Fugger would have preferred, even as early as the middle of the sixteenth century, to liquidate the company whose fate was in his hands. But that was impossible; the firm was too deeply involved in the banking business. In the hope of recovering former loans, new millions were tossed

into the bottomless pit of Habsburg finance. Thus
after the death of Anton in 1560, when the leadership
of the firm had been taken over by his son Markus
and other members of the family, the Fuggers lost the
bulk of their wealth as a result of the bankruptcies
of the national governments, especially the Spanish
and the Dutch of the sixteenth and seventeenth centuries. What remained was chiefly that which, through
the clever family policy of Jacob Fugger the Rich,
had been invested in land, and was thus immune to
the vacillations of mercantile and financial fortune.

During the seventeenth century, the mercantile activity and the importance of the Fuggers was for the
most part lost. Even more complete was the loss of
the great mercantile talent of the family. Anton Fugger himself was far from being the merchant genius
that Jacob the Rich had been. One must not be de-
ceived by the outward brilliance of the family and
the firm during Anton's lifetime. The high point in
the development of the Fugger fortune was definitely
passed not long after the death of Jacob Fugger the
Rich. The words which Thomas Mann used in his
"Buddenbrooks," the story of the decline of a merchant family, apply also to the Fuggers: "I know
something of which you have never thought; I know
it from life and from history, namely that the outward, visible, and tangible symbols of fortune and

prosperity only appear when in truth everything else is on the decline. These outward signs require time to develop, like the light of a star in the heavens of which we cannot be sure, when it most brightly shines, whether it is not already dying away, or is perhaps already extinguished."

LETTERS AND ARTICLES OF ASSOCIATION
1512–1526

1. *Articles of association between Jacob Fugger and his four nephews (30 December, 1512, Augsburg)* [1]

I, Jacob Fugger, burgher of Augsburg, hereby announce and make known to all and sundry that the former Ulrich and George Fugger, my beloved brothers, now deceased, and I for a period of several years carried on our fraternal trade together out of our common capital, and according to the property of each; and to that end we severally made contracts mutually binding upon ourselves, as follows: firstly, articles of association, of the date of 18 August, 1494; secondly, an extension or renewal of the same, dated Friday after the day of Thomas the Apostle in 1502; and thirdly, a contract concerning, among other things, the Hungarian trade, dated Friday after the day of Thomas the Apostle in 1502. These contracts were made in similar terms, and in them we bound ourselves mutually for ourselves and our various heirs in such a way that, if one or two among us three brothers died, the two or one remaining alive among us

1 Jansen, M., *Jacob Fugger der Reiche. Studien und Quellen*, vol. i, pp. 289–295.

should determine for the heirs of the deceased what was their capital and their profit or gain. With this decision the heirs should be entirely satisfied, and should demand no further accounting, nor any other reckoning. Also, when one or two among us died, it should remain the same as though he or they still lived; and the same articles should continue to be in force, and the two or one among us who still lived should govern and act, according to these articles, exactly the same as though we all three still lived.

And it has now come to pass, in accordance with the will of the Almighty, that my two beloved brothers are deceased, namely George on the 14th day of March in 1506, and Ulrich on the 19th day of April in 1510. For that reason, I have now to make an accurate accounting, and an approximate estimate, in accordance with the above-named agreements and articles, to my two deceased brothers' heirs, namely: Frau Anna Fugger of Cremnitz, the wife of the noble and honorable George Thurzo, Chamberlain to His Royal Majesty of Hungary; Frau Ursula Fugger, widow of the deceased honorable knight Philip von Stein; Frau Veronica Fugger, wife of Walther Echinger of Ulm; Frau Sybil, wife of the honorable Hansen Marx of Bubenhofen; and Jungfrau Susan, the five abovementioned being the several daughters of my deceased brother Ulrich, the reckoning being made in view of their paternal and maternal inheritances. Further, to Frau Regina Imhof, bereaved widow of my deceased brother George, for so much as is due her after the death of her husband. Also to the worthy Marcus Fugger, prior at Regensburg, etc.; Frau Regina Fugger Hansen Baumgartner, the wife of the young citizen of Augsburg, both named being the children of my deceased brother George, the reckoning being made on account of their paternal inheritance and property. Further, to the Jungfrau Felicitas Fugger, nun in the Order of Saint Catherine, who during the life of my deceased brother Ulrich has received her share, together with Ulrich and Hieronymus, sons of my deceased brother Ulrich, and Raimund and Anton, sons of my deceased brother George, on account of the paternal and maternal property of my deceased brother Ulrich and his bereaved widow, and the paternal property of my deceased brother George. To all these I must make a distribution and a complete list on account of all the other property of my two above-named deceased brothers, and concerning all this arrange a complete transfer by quittance and in other ways.

For the fraternal association of myself and my two brothers Ulrich and George, in so far as it concerns the common trade, is now ended. In view of all this, and in order that the business begun by us three brothers might the longer continue, and so that our family and name be properly carried on, and my two brothers' sons become familiar with the trade, I have determined to carry on and manage the business myself, and to take industriously in hand my two brothers' sons, namely Ulrich and Hieronymus, sons of my brother Ulrich, and Raimund and Anton, sons of my brother George. I therefore invite them to join me in my common trade and in the Hungarian trade, and hereby do take them in with me in my business, for the six years next following the date of this document, and according to the terms of this agreement, but under no other conditions than the following:

The above-named four, my nephews, shall leave with me in my trade, for profit and loss during the specified time all their capital which is due and owing to them on account of the distribution and of the gain and profit of the trade which their two fathers and I formerly carried on, together with the noble and honorable Hansen and George Thurzo, our brothers-in-law, and otherwise. And this shall have reference to both the landed property and the "Preferred Share." And in my next accounting, which I shall give in the way determined upon by my two deceased brothers and myself in our agreements, they shall accept in their entirety the amounts which I shall allot to them or their heirs, and shall waive all further advances, and shall give me a complete quittance in the matter.

Furthermore shall my above-mentioned four nephews collectively and each in particular recognize and look upon me as the head of this my business, together with such trade as I give them to do and accomplish; they are also faithfully bound to be true and obedient in all things, in whatsoever form and for whatever things this may be required, and to further the trade and business, and to avoid damage and injury to it to the best of their ability, and to hold the business in complete secrecy and tell no one. And the association shall be called *Jacob Fugger und seine Gebrüder Söhne,* or in Italian, *Jacobo Fugger e nepoti.* They, my four above-mentioned nephews, shall also in unison and singly carry on such trade in accordance with my command, and shall do nothing but what I command and give them permission to do. And if I direct one or all of them to do something, and afterward recall it to myself, they shall not dispute it. And what I alone arrange, or bind the association to, to that shall they also none the less be committed, and shall be bound to its accomplishment along with me.

And what the above-named my four nephews collectively or singly shall do, that shall they or he in no way keep secret from me. To that end shall none of them conceal from me the record books or other writings, or their acts, but shall show me all faithfully and without contradiction. The same shall be done by their heirs, should one of them die; and they shall not have the power to enter into trade, nor to seize any writings, nor to conceal or keep them from me.

These my nephews shall further, neither collectively nor singly, carry on any kind of trade, enterprise, or association for themselves, neither among themselves nor with anyone else, without my knowledge and consent. To that end shall none of them, without my knowledge, consent, and desire undertake any kind of responsibility whatever, whether in money or landed property, neither orally, nor in writing, nor in any other way, neither for himself nor among themselves for me or for another outsider; and no matter in what fashion such might take place, it shall nevertheless be entirely void and without force.

Each of my above-named nephews shall also, in my business, render faithfully and truly an account of all his receipts and disbursements and his other dealings, and whatever is lacking in the accounting, he shall make good himself. And whatever any one of them shall for himself require, take, or need, that shall be charged to him. Nevertheless shall none of them without my permission and consent take any considerable amount of money to use for himself, nor take it in any way from the business. When, however, one or more desires money from the business for his need or nourishment, such money I will give and accord to him, but not more than the fourth part of his capital in the six years, but only at one time, and at a time when such payments seem to me to be least disadvantageous or harmful to the business. And the profit and gain for such sums shall then according to reckoning be withheld from him or them.

And since they, my nephews, have not contributed with me in two equal third parts to my Hungarian and other common trade, but I rather have had to contribute the larger share, it shall rest with me, and upon my pleasure, whether I grant and accord to them, for the gain and profit therefrom, anything in excess of their due, and their share in the capital.

And I reserve to myself, and have the right and the full power, in case any of the above-mentioned my four nephews, singly or in several conduct himself or themselves contrary to my pleasure and will or otherwise unfittingly, to dismiss him or them, before the expiration of the six years, or the extension thereof, in the business and the association, without being required to give any cause for my action; or to give them notice within the said six years and before the expiration of the same, or the extension thereof, or at any time that I choose. On the other hand, my nephews shall not have the power, singly or together, to do the same before the expiration of the six years or the extension thereof. And during the six years before the expiration of the same, or after the expiration of the six years, or as I may desire during the six years to dismiss from the trade, or give notice to one or more of my said nephews, or in case one or more dies during the six years or the extension thereof, then or otherwise, whenever I desire, for a long or short period, I shall and will have full power to close up all the business, affairs, and accounts that are then outstanding, and to reckon them up; and when I have thus done and reckoned, to say to them and their heirs how much belongs to each of them or their heirs. And with what I allot or reckon to each of them, or the heirs of the same, they and their heirs shall be entirely satisfied, content, and appeased, without making any controversy, and shall accept that, and shall demand no further accounting nor anything else, but shall accord complete belief to my simple word. And the payment in the said case, both of capital and of profit, to whom it may belong, shall take place in six successive Frankfurt fairs, a sixth part at each fair; but in all the said cases, when the allotment and payment shall take place through me, it shall rest with me whether I' divide and give over to them singly or together, or to the heirs of the same,

debts or goods in making the payment, and how they shall be appraised or valued. And also after notice of the payment has been given, such money shall no longer lie for profit or for loss.

When then the six years have passed and expired, and in the meantime by me alone or after the six years by me and my nephews, the above-mentioned further contract has not been made, or I have not concluded another one with them, then this shall hold another three years after the expiration of the six years; and further, if after the expiration of the said three years, I have not further contracted with them, then it shall continue further. In case I should die in the six years, or during the time of the extension, then my two nephews, Ulrich and Raimund, shall sign my name as it is now done, and shall have the power to carry on the business and the association, to handle money, debts, and goods, as though I were still living, and shall alone do and have all the power and the right which I have toward themselves, their brothers, and their and my heirs to make an accounting, statements, estimates, and deliveries; and shall not be disputed therein by my heirs nor by anyone else, but these shall trust and believe their simple word.

They, my two nephews, Ulrich and Raimund, shall not be hurried by my heirs for what is due to me from the business for capital and profit, but they, my two nephews, shall as stated above between themselves make an accounting and in one year or one and one-half years after my death shall make it known to my heirs, and then, in accordance with the announcement, in three years at six successive Frankfurt fairs shall make complete payment.

In case I alter one or more of the above points or articles, and do it differently, or add anything which concerns this business, whether it is something which I wish to have maintained during my life or after my death between me and my nephews, and my or their heirs, or between themselves and their heirs, on account of the business and trade, whether it be in writing or orally in my business, or my testament or otherwise, in whatever way it may take place, and be planned, arranged, done, established, announced, or declared, then it is my meaning and will that this be held and maintained in preference to the above declaration, and shall be strictly adhered to by my nephews and my and their heirs.

And this contract and agreement, as well as others which I shall make on account of this business, and the documents and contracts which formerly my two deceased brothers, Ulrich and George, and I made with the honorable George Thurzo and his relatives, on account of this business and trade, and also the other documents which have previously been announced by me and my two deceased brothers and now once more by me and my nephews on account of the "Preferred Share" of the Hungarian trade and the landed property, shall all remain uninjured and unimpaired.

All of this, which is said above and declared by me, I promise and bind myself faithfully and freely to maintain truly within the terms of this document, and to carry it out, and to do nothing contrary to it, either myself or through another on my behalf. In proof of which I have given and delivered this document signed with my own hand, to all four of the above-mentioned nephews, sons of my two deceased brothers, and their heirs, and have publicly attached my own seal thereto, and have requested the honorable and wise Ulrich Sultzer, my brother-in-law, and Conrad Rehlinger, the councilor, both burghers of Augsburg, publicly to attach their seals to mine, without prejudice to them and their heirs; and I bind myself unreservedly thereby, so far as this contract bear upon me. The witnesses for my request for the seal are the honorable and wise Hartmann Sultzer, my brother-in-law, and Mathias Langenmantel, both burghers of Augsburg. The same done and given in Augsburg on the thirtieth day of the month of December, in the 1513th year of Christ our dear Lord.

I, Jacob Fugger, burgher of Augsburg, acknowledge in further confirmation all the above with this my own signature, and that this document is thus, with all its contents above described, by me declared, done, and arranged, and is sealed by me and others therein named, on account of my request.[1]

2. *Emperor Maximilian to his government at Innsbruck (20 May, 1515, Augsburg)* [2]

To my noble, honorable, learned, and faithful subjects. Several years since, for excellent reasons, we decided in secret, for our own good, and the good of our House and the House of Austria, upon two marriages between our son and daughter and the daughter and son of King Valdislaw of Hungary and Behaim. In connection therewith we procured a promise that, after the death of said King Vladislaw, until the time when his children came of age, the administration of the Crown of Hungary and Behaim should fall to us. We further determined to draw up the contracts necessary on both sides, and to exchange them; but still to keep the whole arrangement secret. And then we would both meet, so that the arrangement could be made public, and the betrothing of the children to one another be partially carried out, and all the above sworn to by the subjects of both of us.

---

[1] A parchment document in book form, with three seals attached, in the Fugger-Archiv, at Augsburg, 31, 2.

[2] Jansen, *op. cit.*, vol. i, pp. 383–387.

Since then we have treated with our royal brother on various occasions, for the settlement of our meeting place and time, so that the above arrangements might be brought to conclusion. Now for various reasons, this meeting has not taken place; but we considered, nevertheless, how important this matter was for us, and hoped that our brother, the King of Hungary, taking into consideration his age and weakness, might, before his death, be glad to complete the arrangements and to see us personally. Accordingly, we have, with earnest endeavor on both sides, arranged that we and our brother, the King of Hungary, and the King of Poland as well, are to meet in our principality of Austria below the Enns. It is not, however, fitting for our mutual dignity that we ourselves treat of such matters, but it is proper rather that all matters between ourselves and our two brothers be previously arranged and concluded, so that we come together merely to carry on friendly conversation. To this end, we have some time since sent our prince and friend the Cardinal von Gurgk to both of the above-named kings and empowered him to make final arrangements in all matters. Through his industry, most of the arrangements have been concluded, and, when necessary, he has left it to us to arrive at an opinion. We have therefore concluded that our meeting should take place, and that in particular the daughter of the

King of Hungary should be delivered into our hands. When we reached this conclusion, we sent our friend von Gurgk again to both kings at Bresburg, so that he might make final arrangements with them, and provide for a meeting of all three of us with our children.

Now, we have reason to think, in fact, we have knowledge, that our two brothers will come to us with great array of followers, with much regalia and other luxuries, making an imposing appearance. It is, therefore, fitting, in view of the royal meeting, the pledge of marriage, and other mutual contracts and understandings, between us and our children, as well as our two kingdoms and lands, that we also prepare ourselves for their arrival and our meeting, with an imposing array, with princes and other high personages, together with luxurious and expensive jewels and equipment. Furthermore, we must necessarily entertain our royal brothers and their children, as well as the high personages whom they bring with them, using royal regalia, silver plate, and other tokens of honor, when the meeting takes place in our city of Vienna. As you yourselves may imagine, we require for this a considerable sum of money. And however difficult we may think that is to provide, in view of the weary war in which we have long been engaged, and which has so exhausted our treasury, we still think of the good that may come to us, our children, and our House of Austria from such brotherly meetings, marriage contracts, and mutual understandings, and how we thus will put our lands and people at permanent peace with the kingdoms of Hungary, Behaim, Poland, and Märhern. Furthermore, we may secure their aid and assistance against the Venetians, and thus earlier secure an honorable peace from the same Venetians, to the benefit of all our lands.

So, for this and other reasons, we think that the meeting with our brother kings is advantageous, and that it must take place with ceremony, honor, etc., for our sake. Therefore we have arranged for 1,000 horses with harness and equipment, and 1,000 unequipped, together with our costly jewels and articles of luxury, and still not to excess, in view of the coming of our brothers. In addition, we have summoned certain high princes and other people of rank, and are entirely prepared, as soon as our friend the Cardinal has completed his task and notifies us, to move immediately toward Vienna, and await the arrival of our brothers there.

Since, however, we require, as we noted above, for such a procedure a considerable sum of money, and since our treasury is almost exhausted, we must do what we can, and finance ourselves in whatever way is possible.

For this reason, and on the above-mentioned grounds, we have made a financial deal with our counselor, Jacob Fugger, through two letters, which we herewith forward to you. It is fitting that such financing take place with your knowledge, and that the letters concerning it be prepared and worded according to your order.

Now as we know and realize with what considerable sums of money you have formerly helped us from the treasury of your government, and particularly in the support of our *ordinari,* and how as a result our treasury is practically exhausted, we would gladly spare you; nevertheless, you are asked to consider of what importance these agreements are with Hungary, Behaim, and Poland, and in particular the marriage. And more especially since we are well informed that if we do not conclude this matter now, and meet with our royal brothers, that no arrangement will be possible in future, and the marriage will fall through, and the daughter will not be given to us; and furthermore that the two kings, as well as their kingdoms, lands, and people, will become declared enemies of our lands and people, and will ally themselves with the Venetians, strengthening and abetting the latter, so that we will be unable to conclude peace. In addition, we would certainly have the war in our Austrian lands at once; we are, indeed, unable to say to you how disadvantageous and weakening it would be to us if the above-mentioned dealings should fall through. But you can conceive it for yourselves. Therefore we turn to you with this especially earnest request, and remind you, whom we look upon with special confidence, as you well know and realize, how important this whole matter is to us, and what good and benefit may come out of it for us and our children, as well as our lands and people. And for these reasons, we request you to accept the proposed loan with the above-mentioned Fugger, and to sign the above-named contract and letter according to the manner of our treasury, and to affix the seal; and to send it back to us immediately by postal courier, and not to refuse it nor delay with it. For in the gracious trust which we repose in you, we have counted upon this in our financial plans, and have arranged our affairs and departure accordingly, and have so planned for us and our family, and have also sent word to the princes and arranged with them that, so soon as our friend the Cardinal von Gurgk writes that the main agreement with the two kings, and the fact of our meeting have been concluded, we are to move on immediately. But we cannot do this unless the loan from the Fuggers is carried through. For without this we cannot go on, but will have to drop all the above dealings with both kings, and abandon the plan for our and their children, and cancel all the arrangements; and it will probably bring about the disadvantages and injuries suggested above if we finally abandon our meeting with them. If we knew any other method of finance, we would have been only too glad to have spared you this; but we know of no other way. And the matter will bear no delay, for the two kings have already waited long upon us; if we do not now carry it through to completion, they will lose their desire, and it will perhaps give them cause not to want to meet us. Therefore we have been forced to do as we have indicated above, and must move immediately upon receipt of the von Gurgk letter. And when we have completed this Hungarian arrangement, we will then have ways and means of preventing this Fugger loan from being disadvantageous or harmful, or causing any difficulty to our treasury, as we will disclose to you at the proper time. We did not wish to leave you uninformed in the matter. We earnestly request you to further this matter, and not to delay nor to refuse, on account of the necessities above indicated. You will thereby do us a special favor which will be graciously recognized. Given in our and the Imperial City of Augsburg on the 20th day of May in the year etc. xvto.

By His Imperial Majesty and signed by Him.

Do not forsake us in such necessity. For all our welfare depends upon it. p. m. pr. To the government and Council at Innsbruck.[1]

3. *Letter from Emperor Maximilian's two representatives to the Emperor (2 October, 1515, Augsburg)* [2]

Our Most Gracious Emperor. We arrived here on Friday, 28 September, at three P. M.; and as Your Majesty's instructions and letter of credit [?] (*credentzen*) reached us on the following Sunday at two P. M., we thereupon, with utmost zeal, opened negotiations with Jacob Fugger concerning an extension of time on the three points or articles, according to Your Majesty's instructions, and first on behalf of the 12,000 gulden. To this he gave us a detailed answer, namely, that he had extended loans to Your Majesty for some time past, and in this year had given to the smelting works at Rattemberg Schwaz silver and copper, and to Your Majesty's treasury and in other ways had furnished such large sums of money that the total amounted to 300,000 Rhenish gulden. Practically all of this remains as yet unpaid to him, so that he suffers a great lack of ready money, and has had to contract loans among his good friends, which will

[1] A copy at Innsbruck, at the Statthalterei-Archiv. Copy-book I, Series 1515–16 (G9), fol. 33 ff.
[2] Jansen, *op. cit.,* vol. i, pp. 387–391.

have to be repaid out of the income from the above-mentioned deals and loans. With special reference to the 12,000 Rhenish gulden, which are due him at Christmas-time, he has arranged to pay out of that amount the 10,000 gulden which he owes to the treasury at Innsbruck, and which fall due on December 1. In other respects, too, he has made his reckoning with the desire not to be confused in his arranged and ordered payments, and asks to be excused to Your Majesty and your government on account of this loan, so that he may be spared this time, until such time as he has satisfied his creditors, by which time he will have partly raised the above sum of gulden. Otherwise he would not have refused to have extended further loans to Your Imperial Majesty and the officials of the government, as he would like to do with the best will.

He also had not expected, in view of the obedient loan, which he had recently made on the trip from Vienna, with great difficulty and cost, to Your Imperial Majesty, that Your Majesty would so soon seek a further loan—and with other words requested that we, as above stated, should excuse him to Your Imperial Majesty and the gentlemen of the government.

Thereupon we again repeated to him with the greatest justice, and showed him the serious situation and duty which now lay before him, and also the gracious trust reposed in him by Your Imperial Majesty and all your government at Innsbruck, and with other words urged him to consider it all, and said we would come to him again and would hope to receive a better answer from him.

And when we came to him the next day, he clung to his first answer; and thereupon we took up with him, according to our instructions, again with great skill, the other dun, namely that for 58,000 gulden. Thereupon the said Fugger gave us an answer as follows, namely: that to him such dealing was entirely unreasonable, and it would not redound to his credit that one desired discussions and arguments over arranged and concluded contracts, and delay of the payments; he was forced to take into consideration that, if he did this once, and the payment became due again, he would again be involved in discussions and arguments over a delay in payment, and the like, which was not reasonable to him as a merchant, and might indeed involve discredit for the treasury among other merchants who took note of this.

Also it was no part of his intention to put out money simply at interest; it was not right nor advantageous, etc., and in spite of much talk and controversy, he would give no other reply or answer concerning this point. But we again requested of him that he consider it, and that we should come again to him after eating. But he said, he would not refuse us, but he feared he would not be able to think otherwise.

And so we came to him again after luncheon, but he clung to his former answer, repeating all the above-described objections, so that we, according to our instructions, had to bring up the third point, concerning a silver or copper deal, which we then did with the greatest zeal. Thereupon he answered us that while he truly wished to do for the pleasure of Your Imperial Majesty and the government everything which lay in his power, with repetition of his great expenditure and debts, as described above, that the silver was promised to the seventh or eighth and the copper to the fourth year. He also pointed out, with a special complaint, that, although formerly from 12,000 to 14,000 marks of silver had been produced in the smeltery in a year, now, when he had loaned a considerable sum of money on it, not more than 6,000 or 7,000 marks were made in a year, which was a great injury to him, and one that he had not reckoned on. And he did not know how long he would live, or how it might be over a period of years on account of this war. And he had in addition a good deal of negotiating, and it increased daily, so that men now came to him at his house to whom he would willingly have traveled far in years past, which he would like to be rid of. Nevertheless, he had decided, since he was advancing in years and had no children, to carry out the business in which he was now engaged and to refrain from entering upon other long-time deals, and to bring in the debts which were now outstanding, and to pay his creditors, etc. None the less, if he had money, which he did not at this time, or if the matter could be delayed until Easter-time, he expected that in the meantime from the above-mentioned deals and debts perhaps a hundred thousand gold gulden would come in and be paid, so that if propositions were then made to him by His Majesty and his government, which were not too far-reaching, and so that he could look to a definite and certain place from which he would recover his money in time, he would then go into negotiations and gladly do all he could, as he had formerly done for the sake of Your Imperial Majesty and his government alone, and not because of any profit or gain.

He also pointed out to us how we might raise something from other merchants here, several of whom he named to us; he also stated that he had at the present day well over 300,000 gulden of copper deposited in three or four places, of which very little had been sold since the latest copper contract, and that he hoped to bring copper to a higher point than it had ever been.

And although in this matter we intimated to him

more than once that if he knew of any proposition which was reasonable to him, and on the basis of which he would loan money to Your Majesty, he should describe and explain this proposition to us, so that we could make it known to Your Majesty, and ask you to let us know about it, but he did not wish to make us any proposition, but indicated to us that since the silver from the Schwaz and the smelting plant were promised for a long period of years, it would not be reasonable to him to put out money at any interest, and for that reason he truly knew of no plan. He would, however, gladly consider a proposition from us, and if it seemed to him at all acceptable, he would gladly and obediently conduct himself therein as heretofore. Accordingly Your Imperial Majesty and your whole administration should take under consideration, whether and how one or more such propositions could be formed, and graciously let us know by the earliest post. And we should act therein to the height of our capacity and enterprise.

And since Your Imperial Majesty's instructions required us to notify you of the dealings we had with the Fugger, together with all our advice and counsel, although our advice in the matter is slight, still we think, if the proposition is made to the Fugger in the nature of a contract or otherwise, with good security, but not with interest, nor too circuitous nor too long drawn out, he should within a short time after the making of the contract have ready a sum of money, and more later, even though in his reply he refuses Easter as a date. For as Your Imperial Majesty informed us at the conclusion of our instructions, if Fugger wished to do neither the one nor the other, that we should deal further with the Hochstetters and other merchants, we none the less wish to open the negotiations in the meantime with the Höchstetters, and whether we are successful or not, later turn to other merchants. And still we do not wish to deal too soon or too suddenly with them upon the credit of Your Majesty, unless we find that something worth while can be thereby secured. In the meantime, and before we negotiate something explicitly with other merchants, we hope Your Majesty will notify us about this matter of the Fugger, so that we know how to conduct ourselves.

In case, however, that we, before we receive an answer from Your Imperial Majesty concerning this notice of ours about the Fugger, make some definite deal with other merchants, we will make it known to Your Majesty by day-and-night post; although the treasurer fears that we will make no deal and find no large sum of money with other merchants than the

Fuggers, we wish nevertheless to make our modest efforts therein with the best means.

And we hereby commend ourselves obediently to Your Imperial Majesty. Dated at Augsburg on Thursday the 2nd of October at the eleventh hour in the night. Anno domini etc. xv.

Your Imperial Majesty's

Humble

BLASI HÖLTZL

JOHANN ZOTT [1]

4. A letter from Jacob Fugger to the Elector Frederick of the Pfalz (22 August, 1522, Augsburg)

Your Serene Highness and Highborn Prince, and Gracious Lord, my humble service is always at the command of Your Princely Grace.

Your Princely Grace well remembers that you are to pay to the Company Rem and in part to me at the Frankfurt autumn fair the fourth part of the 14,000 Rhenish gulden, that is, 3,500 gulden in gold. It is therefore my humble request to Your Grace that you bear this debt in mind, and arrange to pay, at the specified time, this sum to Andreas Rem and his Company. It is my humble request that this be done. I hereby humbly recommend myself to Your Princely

[1] A copy at Innsbruck, at the Statthalterei-Archiv, Maximiliana XII, 40.

Grace. Dated Augsburg on the 22nd day of the month of August, 1522.

> Your Serene Highness'
> Humble
> JACOB FUGGER [1]

5. *Charles* v *takes under his protection the mining interests of the Fuggers* (*26 October, 1525, Toledo*) [2]

We, Charles v, etc., hereby give notice to all and sundry that Jacob Fugger, beloved subject of us, our council, and our empire, has brought to our notice how he and his two deceased brothers' sons on several occasions and in particular on two occasions made two deals and contracts, namely: firstly, a four-year contract for himself and the above-mentioned two brothers' sons, made the 7th day of November of the year 1514, which went into effect at Christmas-time of the year 1516; and secondly a four-year contract with Ambrose and Hansen Höchstetter, together with their relatives, made on the 30th day of the month of October in the year 1515, to go into force at the expiration of the above-mentioned first four years. According to these contracts, the Schwaz silver and copper in our Duchy of Tyrol belonging to the former

---

[1] A copy is in the Bischöfliches Archiv, Eichstadt.
[2] Jansen, *op. cit.*, vol. i, pp. 404–406.

worshipful Emperor Maximilian of blessed memory, our forefather, and to no one else, was to go to them. And how, more than forty years before and earlier, in the time of the above-named Emperor Maximilian our forefather, and our beloved cousin the Archduke Sigmund of Austria, of blessed memory, on account of the above-mentioned Schwaz copper and silver and the mines as well as the smelteries, and for the maintenance of the same and for their use, every year contracts with various merchants were made without harm, sometimes for silver alone, and sometimes for silver and copper. And that he and his brothers' sons had had dealings with such contracts, as well as with their own silver and copper, which they had secured from their own property and mines which they bought in our Austrian lands and in the kingdom of Hungary. And that they had ever dealt and acted legally and justly, as honest people, and had been recognized as such by everybody. But concerning all this it has reached them that he and his brothers' sons were accused, not only of making their deal with our forefather, Emperor Maximilian, on account of the Schwaz silver and copper, but also of dealing in and transporting the same, as well as the silver and copper belonging to Jacob Fugger and his brothers' sons, which they obtained from their own property and mines in our Austrian lands as well as in Hungary;

and of having done all this contrary to law, and of having thereby caused and brought about to their advantage an increase in the price of silver and copper, contrary to the general good and welfare. All of which they entirely deny, having shown us rather, in all humility, what they have accomplished by the purchase of the above-mentioned silver and copper; and that this had been done not otherwise than with the consent of the Roman Emperor and that it was properly in force, and legitimate. And that he and his brothers' sons have not endeared prices nor dealt illegally, neither with the silver and copper bought from His Imperial Majesty, nor with the other which they secured from their own mines in our Austrian lands. And that much less have they brought about in the German nation any enhancement of prices, such as is condemned by law, or is unseemly or criminal. For it is true and may be ascertained that he and his brothers' sons not only sold most of the silver and copper which they had bought in German lands, but also that the silver of eight, ten, twelve, and sixteen years before, that is, before they had bought the above-named silver from Emperor Maximilian, had been worth rather more than less than it now was, and that forty, thirty, and twenty-four years before the copper was bought by the merchants of the Schwaz at about as much per centner as it is now;

and that he and his brothers' sons in obedience to the law, without any hindrance or prohibition had always acted and dealt reasonably, and still did. More especially as they had transported, dealt, and otherwise traded in, in Germany and in other lands and nations, their own property and goods such as gold, silver, copper, and other metals, which they had during many years secured from their own mines and property in foreign kingdoms as in Hungary, and which they had often bought from no one else; and from which Almighty God had hitherto granted them a good part of their nourishment, since they otherwise paid the customary tolls and dues, through which the rulers and the lands and people have no small benefit in their yearly income; and had done and conducted themselves in the best and most useful way. In all this, they humbly petition and request us to grant him and his brothers' sons our imperial freedom, grace, protection, manifesto, and other necessary legal assistance through further ordinances, statutes, and confirmations, and also in all other ways to guard, protect, and defend them from unfair accusations in everything as above described.

We decree as above, and declare all the above dealings to be legal. . . . Given in our city of Toledo in Castile on the 26th day of the month of October in the 1525th year after the birth of Christ our dear

Lord, in the seventh year of our Roman Empire, and the tenth year of the other.

On the back: Taxa florenos rhen. quadraginta. Ad mandatum caesaree ac catholice Majestatis proprium Brantner.

GENEALOGICAL TABLE OF THE OLDEST AUGSBURG FUGGERS

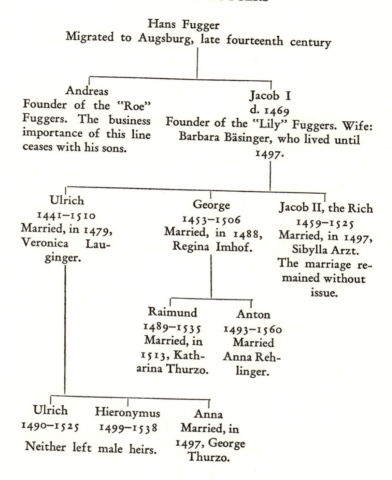

Hans Fugger
Migrated to Augsburg, late fourteenth century

Andreas
Founder of the "Roe"
Fuggers. The business
importance of this line
ceases with his sons.

Jacob I
d. 1469
Founder of the "Lily" Fuggers. Wife:
Barbara Bäsinger, who lived until
1497.

Ulrich
1441–1510
Married, in 1479,
Veronica Lau-
ginger.

George
1453–1506
Married, in 1488,
Regina Imhof.

Jacob II, the Rich
1459–1525
Married, in 1497,
Sibylla Arzt.
The marriage re-
mained without
issue.

Raimund
1489–1535
Married, in
1513, Kath-
arina Thurzo.

Anton
1493–1560
Married
Anna Reh-
linger.

Ulrich
1490–1525

Hieronymus
1499–1538

Neither left male heirs.

Anna
Married, in
1497, George
Thurzo.

BIBLIOGRAPHY

Following is a list of the more exhaustive works on Fugger history which have been used in the preparation of this volume.

1. Richard Ehrenberg, *Das Zeitalter der Fugger. Geldkapital und Kreditverkehr im 16. Jahrhundert.* 2 vols., Jena, 1896. There have been several new editions without changes, and a translation of part into English.

2. Aloys Schulte, *Die Fugger in Rom, 1495–1523. Mit Studien zur Geschichte des kirchlichen Finanzwesens jener Zeit.* 2 vols., Leipzig, 1904.

3. Max Jansen, *Die Anfänge der Fugger (bis 1494).* Leipzig, 1907.

4. Max Jansen, *Jacob Fugger der Reiche. Studien und Quellen I.* Leipzig, 1910.

5. Thea Düvel, *Die Gütererwerbungen Jacob Fuggers des Reichen (1494–1525) und seine Standeserhöhung.* Munich and Leipzig, 1913.

6. Konrad Haebler, *Die Geschichte der Fuggerschen Handlung in Spanien.* Weimar, 1897.

7. Jakob Strieder, *Die Inventur der Firma Fugger aus dem Jahre 1527.* Tübingen, 1905.

8. Jakob Strieder, *Studien zur Geschichte kapitalistischer Organisationsformen. Monopole, Kartelle und Aktiengesellschaften im Mittelalter und zu Beginn der Neuzeit.* Munich and Leipzig, 1914. Second enlarged edition.

9. Ludwig Scheuermann, *Die Fugger als Montanindustrielle in Tirol und Kärnten.* Munich and Leipzig, 1929.

10. Philip Maria Halm, *Adolf Daucher und die Fuggerkapelle bei St. Anna in Augsburg.* Munich and Leipzig, 1921. Valuable for Fugger's relation to art.

The works listed by Jansen, Düvel, and Halm appear in the *Studien zur Fuggergeschichte,* formerly edited by Jansen and now by the present author.

INDEX

223

mel, 31, Ehem, 31, Grander trading company, 40, Höchstetter, 20, 31, 127, 131, 132, 203, 215, Meuting Company, 28, 40, 41, 43, Ravensburg Company, 28, 29, 48, Andreas Rem Company, 214, Rothschilds, 11, 20, 21, 54, 139, 181, Rott, 20, Welser, 60, 97, 98, 148 ff., 156, 167, Welser-Vöhlin House, 40, 42. *See also* South German merchants

Italian, 4, 5, 9, 102, 152, 156, 158, 162, 164, 165, Bardi, 6, Cahorsines, 2, Lombards, 2, 6, Medici, 6, 7, 15, 93, 158, 165, Peruzzi, 6, Strozzi, 7, Tuscan, 6, 7

Francis I of France, 140, 146, 147, 148, 150

Frederick III, 55, 57

Frederick, Elector of the Pfalz, 214

Fugger, Andreas, 52, 53

Anna, 118, 190

Anton, 20, 21, 22, 55, 79, 83, 86, 102, 139, 182, 183, 184, 191, 192

Widow Barbara, 53, 54, 59, 60, 61, 67

Felicitas, 191

George, 23, 54, 56, 57, 58, 61, 63, 65, 71, 76, 86, 88, 118, 176, 189, 190, 191, 198

Hans, 52

Hieronymus, 79, 83, 84, 191, 192

Jacob I, 52, 53, 59, 67

Jacob the Rich, benevolence, 175, 176, business reputation, 155, 156, 157, a captain of industry, 106, 119, an early capitalistic entrepreneur, xvii, xxii, 169, 179, as entrepreneur, 1, 18, 19, 20, 21, 39, 42, 49, 168, Italian inheritance, xviii, 1, 10, 15, 22, 26, opposition to him, 167, 169, 170, 171, 173, 174, prebendary, 54, 61, Venetian apprenticeship, 62, 113

Markus, 184

Raimund, 22, 55, 79, 80, 81, 82, 83, 118, 148, 191, 192, 196

Regina Imhof, 191

Susan, 190

Sybil, 190

Ulrich, 23, 54, 55, 56, 57, 61, 62, 63, 65, 67, 71, 76, 80, 86, 88, 118, 139, 158, 176, 189, 190, 191, 198

Ulrich, Jr., 79, 80, 81, 82, 83, 148, 191, 192, 196

Ursula, 190

Veronica, 190

Fugger agreement of 1494, 62, 63, 68, 70, agreement of 1512, 78, 79, 80, 81

articles of association of 1494, 189, of 1502, 189, of 1512, 189 ff.

branches, 16, 64, 102, 104, 125, 134, 141, 159

business, xii, 56, "common Hungarian trade," 84, 116, 118, 119, 123, 143, 189, 192, 195, geographical extent, 56, 101, 104, 158, 159, in Antwerp, xi, 97, 101, 102, 103, 122, 169, in Augsburg, xi, in Naples, xi, in Rome, 159, in Venice, 97, 103, 104, 111, 122, 125, policy, xiii, 58, 68, 69, 84, 91, 141, 210, 211, "Preferred Share," 72, 74, 82, 83, 192, 199

capital, 63, 64, 86, 89, 183

chapel, 23, 24

coat of arms, 55, 56

Company, 20, 29, 58, 62, 63, 65, 71, 83, 86, 109, 116, 118, 119, 123, 125, 126, 127, 134, 136, 138, 148, 158, 159, 169, 182, 183

Contract of 1502, 68, 70, 71, 73, 74, 76, 77, 79, 81, 189

coparceny, 67, 68

factories. *See* branches